Bridges to Holiness

A Spirituality for Today

Louis G. Miller, C.SS.R.

Liguori Publications
One Liguori Drive
Liguori, Missouri 63057
(314) 464-2500

Imprimi Potest:
Edmund T. Langton, C.SS.R.
Provincial, St. Louis Province
Redemptorist Fathers

Imprimatur:
St. Louis, October 11, 1978
+ John N. Wurm, S.T.D., Ph.D.
Vicar General, Archdiocese of St. Louis

Photo Credits

Orville Andrews:	pp. 18, 19, 28
Marne Breckensiek:	pp. 6, 17, 45, 50, 108, 120
Ewing Galloway:	pp. 64, 78
Wallowitch:	pp. 30, 62, 92, 96

COVER DESIGN: JIM CORBETT
PHOTO: CAMERIQUE

Dedication

This is a community book.

It is about community and the new insights on that important side of human life that have been granted to us in our time.

And it grew out of community: the group of Redemptorist priests and Brothers who joined in a publishing venture in 1947 at Liguori, Missouri, near the city of St. Louis.

I was a member of that community from the beginning, and participated in the ongoing effort we had to make to understand and to reflect in our apostolate the exciting process of renewal in the Church during Vatican II, the great event of the sixties, and developments which have followed it.

The ideas expressed here were forged in many meetings, formal and informal, and countless conversations during those years.

My dedication of the book, therefore, is to the confreres I lived with and worked with at Liguori. My association with them was a singular blessing for which I am grateful to God.

TABLE OF CONTENTS

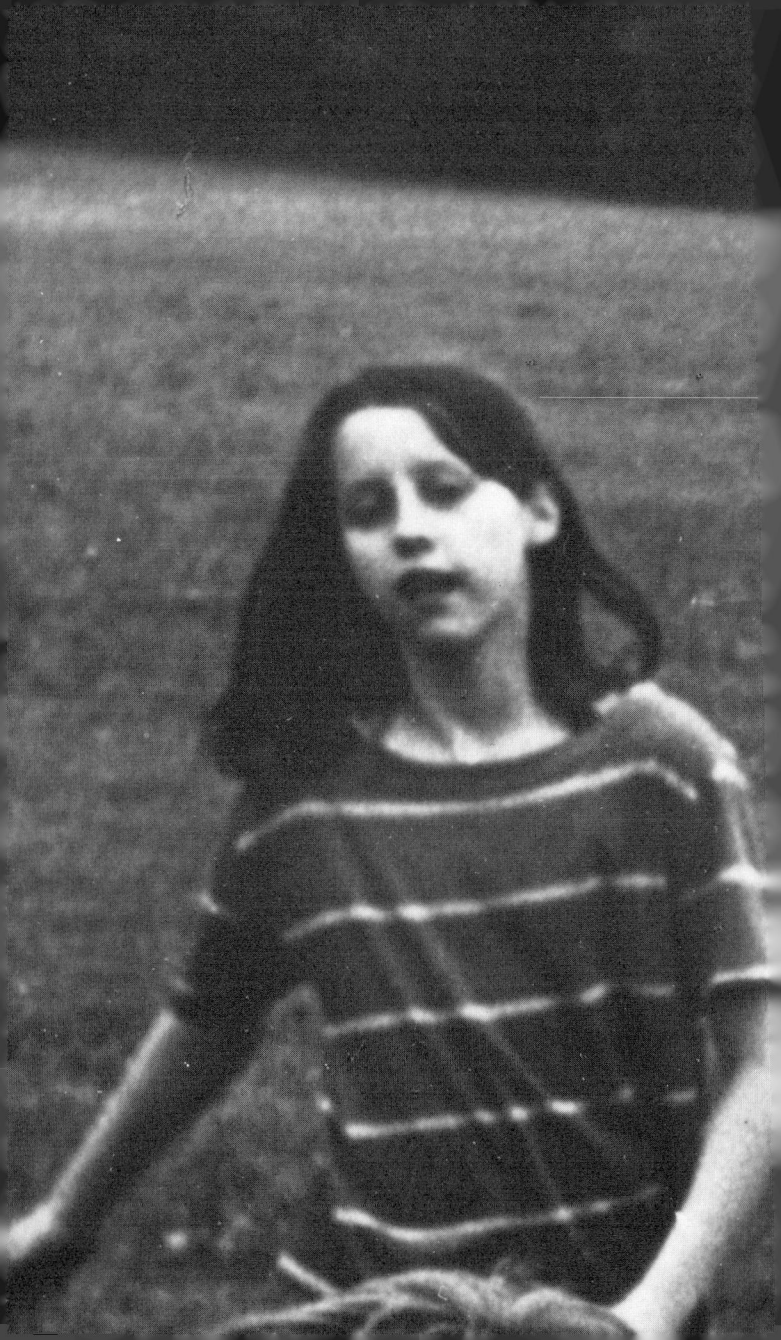

Prologue

There is a story about Laura, a little orphanage girl about 10 years old who was very shy and diffident. Perhaps it was because she had an unsightly red birthmark on the side of her face, and sometimes her companions, with the thoughtlessness of children, made fun of her for this. In any case, she seemed to prefer to be by herself.

But one day a teacher in the orphanage, unobserved, saw the little girl climbing upon the wire fence that enclosed the grounds. Then she reached over and tucked an envelope into a partially loose piece of bark on a tree that grew just on the other side, in the "outside world."

The teacher waited until the little girl was out of sight, then, unable to restrain his curiosity, reclaimed the envelope. In it was a note in a childish scrawl:

"To anybody who reads this, I love you! Laura."

This is a book based on the premise that today, more than in the past, we are being impelled and called to reach out to the Lauras of this world: all those individuals young or old, who, rightly or wrongly, feel unloved.

You hear some people say that they are sick of hearing the word love. They may give vent to their feelings by muttering: "I'm tired of hearing all that talk about love, as if it were the only important thing in life. What about the Ten Commandments? Aren't they important too?"

They certainly are. But if you were to draw up a list of priorities as Christ saw them, you would have to put love in the top position. When he was asked what, in his opinion, was the most important commandment, he did not answer by citing one of the traditional ten. He said: The most important commandment is to love God and love your neighbor.

And on the night before he died, in the solemn moment of leave-taking, he said to his close friends:

This is my commandment:
love one another
as I have loved you (John 15:12).

PERSON-TO-PERSON

We have always accepted this, of course, as an abstract truth. And there have never been wanting those who made it come alive by their personal dedication to deeds of charity: heroic men and women like St. Vincent de Paul, St. John Bosco, and St. Elizabeth Seton.

The difference lies in this: Their spirit of charity has emerged as the common and proper spirit of our time, recognized as such even when, through human frailty, we fail to reflect it.

If you were to ask what is distinctive about today's spirituality as compared to yesterday's, the answer might well be that we feel drawn today to put renewed emphasis on the person-to-person relationship of love.

A spirituality, the way a person relates to God, cannot change in its essential thrust and goal from one age to another: through Christ, in Christ, with Christ to bring each person to the highest possible degree of maturity in the love of God and neighbor. But in this changing world of human circumstances, each generation is drawn to emphasize a different aspect of this central truth.

It is not to pass judgment on the past, but simply to admit reality, that asceticism in a former age seemed to be more concerned with virtues in the abstract, with laws conceived and presented in a logical, objective pattern, lacking, it might be said, in blood and warmth. Canon Law is important, but it surely does not have the paramount importance some were inclined to give it in those years.

Renewal in the Church, responding to a deep reassessment of values in the human spirit, has reestablished the true focus and perspective. It has come home to us, with increasing clarity, that to respond to Christ as a person and to my neighbor as a person in whom Christ lives, I cannot possibly continue to look upon him or her simply as a name, a number, or a "case" out there in the gray areas of life beyond my immediate concern. I must in fact love that person with the same kind of love that Christ showed to me.

THIRST FOR UNDERSTANDING

Love is not a product you can purchase in a store. There are many different kinds of Lauras in the world and many pressing needs, spiritual and physical, that your neighbor has as a unique individual, thirsting for understanding and loving care. How beautifully those needs are set before us in St. Matthew's account of the final Judgment:

For I was hungry and you gave me food,
I was thirsty and you gave me drink.
I was a stranger and you welcomed me,
naked and you clothed me.
I was ill and you comforted me,
in prison and you came to visit me (Matthew 25:35-36).

And to those who wondered how and where they could have met Christ, the answer of the Judge rings out clear and challenging down through the centuries:

"I assure you, as often as you did it for one of my least brothers, you did it for me" (Matthew 25:40)

This book will be concerned with the various ways in which we are called upon to show our love of God and neighbor, the various kinds of persons, one might say, that we are called upon to be:

bridgebuilders between old and young, new ways and old ways,

healers, particularly of bitterness and wounds of the spirit,

pioneers, strong and unafraid in new ventures of the Spirit,

creators of community, striving for the welfare of all,

contemplatives, with warm hearts for
humanity,
disciples, seeking with humility the guidance
of the Spirit,
spiritual astronauts, convinced that Christ's
way will prevail.

We can never hope to be all of these kinds of
persons completely. Our human inadequacy will
always fall short of the ideal. But then we think of
Moses, that great and heroic Old Testament
figure whose destiny it was to lead the people of
God out of slavery and to the Promised Land. Like
the rest of us, he had plenty of doubts and
worries and uncertainties. After Yahweh had
spoken to him out of the burning bush and told
him clearly what he was to do, and even worked
several signs and wonders to show his power,
Moses continued to hesitate.

The scene is dramatically set forth in Exodus,
Chapter 4: ". . . in the past, nor recently, nor now
that you have spoken to your servant; but I am
slow of speech and tongue" (Exodus 4:10).

But the Lord refused to accept Moses' excuse
and brushed aside all his objections with the
words:

" 'Go, then! It is I who will assist you in
speaking and will teach you what you are to say.'
Yet he insisted, 'If you please, Lord, send
someone else!' " (Exodus 4:12-13)

ONE OF A KIND

How human his response and how typical of
our response, often, to the demands that love
makes upon us. You and I do not have the kind of
job that was assigned to Moses. His was a

responsibility of such importance that the fate of God's people turned upon it.

And yet it is true to say that every human being has a potential gift for the world that is unique and irreplaceable, simply because every human being is entirely unique. Out of all the billions of people in this world, there is not one who is an exact carbon copy of you who are reading these lines. There is not one with exactly the same combination of characteristics and attitudes, the same distinctive temperament and personality.

But if in God's providence you are made unique in this way, then it follows that you are meant to reach out and touch certain hearts with your love in a way that no one else can reach out and touch them. If you do not accomplish your special task, no one else will, because no one else has the special key to those hearts.

Moses had his share of human faults and frailties. He was timid. At times his faith was weak, as when he doubted that the Lord could supply water for his thirsty people. He could be carried away by his feelings and emotions, as when he rose up in wrath and shattered the tablets on which the Ten Commandments were inscribed, when he saw his people worshiping the golden calf.

But there is much consolation also in the fact that God, who knows our human frailty and is merciful, never gave up on Moses. He loved him even in his frailty, and what a beautiful testimony to God's love is found in the last lines of Deuteronomy:

"Since then no prophet has arisen in Israel like Moses, whom the Lord knew face to face. He had no equal in all the signs and wonders the Lord sent him to perform..." (Deuteronomy 34:10-11).

This book is concerned with the signs and wonders of love that it is possible for anyone to perform today, provided he or she is open to the moving of the Spirit and possesses the good will to follow where the Spirit leads.

ANGEL OF PEACE

Cardinal John Henry Newman had a deep conviction, expressed often in his wonderfully perceptive sermons, that God creates every human being to do some definite service, some specific task which he commits to no one else. We may never know in this life what our special task is, but we shall be told it in the world to come.

As Newman expressed it, each of us is a link in a chain, a bond of connection between persons. If I keep his commandments and follow the guiding light of conscience, I shall, even while not directly intending it, do his work; I shall be an angel of peace, a preacher of truth in my own special circumstances of life.

After developing this thought, Newman ends with a beautiful expression of confidence in God:

Therefore will I trust Him,
whatever, wherever I am;
I can never be thrown away.
If I am in sickness
my sickness may serve Him;
if I am in sorrow,
my sorrow may serve Him.
He does nothing in vain.
He knows what He is about.

13

He may take away my friends,
He may throw me among strangers,
He may make me feel desolate,
make my spirits sink,
hide my future from me
still He knows what He is about.

Only love can bring us to the acceptance of the sacrifices God may ask of us in his service and in the service of our neighbor.

But perfect love can make sacrifice a joy.

Three Minute Meditation

Bright and Joyous Love

You have visited the land and watered it;
  greatly have you enriched it.
God's watercourses are filled;
  you have prepared the grain.
*(Lord, drench the dry furrows of my soul with
your love, level the stiff ridges of my selfishness,
ridges which block the flow of my love.)*
Thus have you prepared the land:
      drenching its furrows,
breaking up its clods,
Softening it with showers,
    blessing its yield.
*(Lord, soften the hard clumps
    of my stubborn faults,
melt them with showers of your gentle mercy.
Bless my first fruits,
the timid beginnings of my loving response.)*

You have crowned the year with your
     bounty,
   and your paths overflow with a rich
     harvest;
The untilled meadows overflow with it,
   and rejoicing clothes the hills.
(Lord, let the hillsides of my heart,
   facing the sun,
be wrapped in bright and joyous love.)
The fields are garmented with flocks
   and the valleys blanketed with grain.
   They shout and sing for joy.
(Lord, let my fields be garmented
   in flocks of sheep,
   my loving thoughts and actions,
my valleys be clothed in golden wheat,
   the harvest of my loving service.
Then, Lord, what shouts of joy!
   what singing in my heart!)
                         Psalm 65:10-14

CHAPTER 1

Bridges and Bridgebuilders

There was a time when St. Paul and his erstwhile missionary companion, a young man named John Mark, could not stand the sight of each other.

The reality clearly appears in the Acts of the Apostles.

Paul and Barnabas were commissioned by the church in Antioch, under the inspiration of

the Holy Spirit, to undertake a missionary journey to other lands and other peoples. They decided to take with them the youthful John Mark, whose mother's house in Jerusalem was a gathering place for the early Christians. Peter took refuge there upon his miraculous release from prison (see Acts 12:12).

The missionary team went first to the island of Cyprus and preached there with some success. Then they boarded ship and sailed to the coast of Asia Minor, now Turkey. But at this point, the author of the Acts informs us laconically: "John left them and returned to Jerusalem" (Acts 13:13).

We are not informed as to why he decided to desert the expedition. Was it a personality

conflict? Was Paul too authoritarian for a young man's taste? Were the difficulties of travel, the homesickness, more than Mark had bargained for?

In any case, Paul was much upset, and Mark's departure rankled with him for some time. When later on a second missionary journey was being planned, Barnabas once more wanted to take along his nephew Mark. "But Paul insisted that, as he had deserted them at Pamphylia, refusing to join them on that mission, he was not fit to be taken along now. The disagreement which ensued was so sharp that the two separated. Barnabas took Mark along with him and sailed for Cyprus" (Acts 15:38-39).

There is a pleasant sequel to the story. Paul and Mark (and surely Barnabas as well) were reconciled along the way. Years later, writing to Timothy from the loneliness of his prison in Rome, Paul had a special request: "Get Mark and bring him with you, for he can be of great service to me" (2 Timothy 4:11).

BRIDGING THE GAP

This chapter is about the importance of becoming a bridgebuilder and of consenting to be a bridge. The dispute between Paul and Barnabas and Mark illustrates the difficulty of cooperative effort and, at the same time, encourages us in finding a solution. Age difference surely was a factor in that early Christian dispute, and it is a factor, but not the only one, in the problems of communication and cooperation today.

In this time of cultural change the need for bridgebuilding is crucial. A spirituality for today accepts the challenge joyfully, and matures in the very act of responding to it.

FIRM FOUNDATION

To become an effective bridgebuilder between differing segments of society some conditions have to be fulfilled:

First, you must anchor your bridge on both sides of the cultural river. On one side, the foundation must be based on the enduring sacred realities that have been revealed: that there is a God who created us, loves us, sent his Son to redeem us, asks us freely to respond to his love and obey his law, and wants us to give our loyalty to and share our prayer life with the Church that Christ founded.

But your bridge must find a footing also on the other side of the river, the side that opens out into thick forest and uncharted mountain land. Waiting there to be explored are new problems and new challenges that will require constant adjustment and adaptation. For those of middle years and beyond, the more difficult task is to find a footing on this new and unknown and perhaps rocky and uneven ground.

For the young, the challenge is to keep in good repair the entrance to the bridge that rests on solid and sacred traditions of the past, lest the ultimate meaning of life itself be lost. But everyone, young or old, has the potential to be a bridgebuilder, concerned with finding and uniting all whom the circumstances of our time tend to divide.

SOARING STRUCTURE

A good bridge is in a state of perfect suspension. And the times call for something like a state of suspension in our minds, in response to the ferment and change around us.

A well-constructed bridge seems to be floating in air, as light and graceful as a spider web. Actually, architects and engineers have carefully checked and rechecked the stresses and strains, and the soaring structure has a rocklike stability.

A spirituality suited to today must have something of the same paradoxical combination: free and floating, and yet firmly based on the central absolutes of our relationship with God.

As to the number of these absolutes, one can only say that the number has greatly diminished in the last three decades. Some have been lost along the way; others have withdrawn into the grayness of predawn, and their outline is not as sharply etched as it once was. We were too inclined in past years to invoke infallibility for our opinions. To say this is not to concede that it has become impossible to find truth and that all truth is a matter of opinion.

SWAY FACTOR

For many people, this is a very difficult time in which to live. The renewal in the Church causes them anguish for the very reason that it seems to be so open-ended. There are so many options, so many conflicting opinions.

For example, you hear people complain: "Why do they offer so many different ways to participate in the Mass? Why not settle on one simple mode of procedure and be done with it?"

Or they ask: "Why can't we get clear guidance in so many moral problems that beset us?"

But it is in the very nature of this time of renewal that we must learn to live with a certain measure of uncertainty and openendedness. There are still fixed points: moral principles to guide us, clearly stated by the Church. But just as a bridge, firmly fixed and founded on both sides of the river it spans, must also have a built-in sway factor if it is to survive strong winds, so there must be a sway factor built into our religious and spiritual life. Then, even though we may creak and groan with the tension being put upon the cables, we will be able to withstand any storm.

To be stiff with anger and constantly tense about all change and about every unorthodox moral opinion someone may express is surely to risk collapse and disaster in this era when the strong wind of cultural change is blowing ruthlessly through all our human institutions.

WALKWAY

A good bridge must be content to be stepped on and driven over. That is what a bridge is for.

Let your imagination construct a scene in which two communities, one on each side of a flowing river, are at odds with each other. Perhaps there has been a long history of misunderstanding and real and imagined slights.

There are two ways to go. Each community can station its representative on the river bank and shout insults at the rival group on the opposite shore. Inevitably, insults are shouted back. And nothing happens to further the coming together of both communities to discuss matters of common interest and concern.

But what a service we could perform for these people if we had it in our power to build a bridge over the river which separated them, a bridge over which representatives from both sides could walk with confidence and come to know each other better — thus working together for the common good.

Symbolically, everyone has the potential to build such a bridge, to be such a bridge.

Who can predict what impact on the future will be made by the generation just coming to maturity? Young people themselves do not know what they can and will accomplish in the new world which is being born. Youth, as is well known, tends to be impatient; youth can be sharp, tactless, inconsiderate, ruthless in impaling the hypocrisies of their elders.

And by the same token, those of middle years and beyond can be inconsiderate, unsympathetic, and unresponsive to the idealism of youth, which they themselves may have long lost. They may have minds which are completely closed to new ideas and better ways of doing things.

The human condition being what it is, neither side of the river has a monopoly on either faults or virtues. But it should perhaps be noted that, if you are of the older generation, maturity has possibly, but not necessarily, brought you a certain degree of tolerance, of patience with the foibles of others, of salutary diminishment of the tendency to be so cocksure about your opinions. You can scarcely expect to find in youth what it took you so many years to gain; and indeed, perhaps your gain has not been all that great.

Not in a patronizing way, but with genuine charity, both sides in any dispute must be willing to concede points even while expressing convictions. When you have built your bridge, you should not be dismayed if people are inclined to walk over it; that is what a bridge is for: to remain calm and steady and sturdy even when it is being stepped on.

The Mississippi and the other great rivers of our country have hundreds of bridges along their lengths. But we are in short supply of the kind of symbolic bridge that unites people and allows peacemakers to cross back and forth and arrange for further mutual support.

You may be the kind of person who is qualified to serve this wonderful purpose. And your growth in spirituality will depend on how generously you respond.

BRIDGE IN BALANCE

For some people, balance savors of colorless neutrality and unwillingness to take a stand. But balance need not imply weakness. And surely the word signifies something quite other than the meaning conveyed by the word "mediocrity."

Once again, consider the structure of a good bridge. It possesses a dynamic kind of balance. The stresses and strains of the structure have been well calculated, and the approaches on both sides of the river are firmly anchored.

What does balance in today's spirituality imply?

It means exercising discernment in making choices, and giving proper weight to contrasting kinds of responsibility and reality:

    individual growth and community welfare
    liturgical celebration and private reflective
      prayer

authority and private conscience
personal asceticism and apostolic service
reverential awe and joyous informality
joy at one's redemption and sorrow for one's
    sins
trust in God's mercy and dread of his justice
being in the world and yet not of the world.
It means believing that Christ is present in Word and Sacrament, and also seeing him present in the poor.

There is, moreover, the added challenge that for genuine community growth, in any plan or project that brings people together, a consensus must be sought from individuals of differing temperament, education, environment, and motivation.

Some are introverts and others extroverts.

Some are quick and some are slow.

Some are poets and some are pragmatists.

Some are leaders and some are followers.

What a beautiful challenge it is to build bridges between all these contrasting types.

The forming of a genuine spirit of community is commonly thought to be one of the major needs of our time. In the past our culture tended to isolate people in their individualism. It is an insight that surely comes from the Holy Spirit that a true collegial approach to problems is possible, bringing together in the search for consensus individuals in all the wonderful diversity of their make-up and background.

LIFT TO THE HEART

"Blessed are the peacemakers," Christ said. Today he might have added: "Blessed are the bridgebuilders!"

It lifts the heart to see the massive yet graceful structures that span our great rivers in all parts of the nation, seemingly floating on air despite their giant size.

People who build bridges for peace lift the heart even more. Without doubt, that is what brought the Nobel peace prize to two women in Northern Ireland, a Protestant and a Catholic, who in that troubled land dared to stand united before their rival groups and say:

"Peace is the concern of everybody, and we want everybody to be involved in restoring and maintaining it."

Such an action surely is an answer to the prayer of Christ, and challenges you to look for ways to be peacemakers and bridgebuilders in the circumstances of your lives:

I pray . . . that all may be one
as you, Father, are in me, and I in
    you;
I pray that they may be [one] in us,
that the world may believe that you
    sent me.
. . . and that you loved them as you loved
    me (John 17:20-23).

Christ went out of the supper room and submitted to a cruel death to prove his love.

You have the easier task: to build bridges, so that the unity he prayed for can become a reality.

Your growth in spirituality depends upon it.

Harbinger of Peace

[Our] mission requires us first of all to create in the Church itself mutual esteem, reverence and harmony, and acknowledge all legitimate diversity; in this way all who constitute the one people of God will be able to engage in ever more fruitful dialogue, whether they are pastors or other members of the faithful. For the ties which unite the faithful together are stronger than those which separate them: let there be unity in what is necessary, freedom in what is doubtful, and charity in everything . . . .

We are also mindful that the unity of Christians is today waited and longed for by many nonbelievers. For the more this unity is realized in truth and charity under the powerful impulse of the Holy Spirit, the more it will be a harbinger of unity and peace throughout the whole world.

Let us, then, join our forces and modify our methods in a way suitable and effective today for achieving this lofty goal, and let us pattern ourselves daily more and more after the spirit of the Gospel, and work together in a spirit of brotherhood to serve the human family which has been called to become in Christ Jesus the family of the sons of God.

The Church Today, 92

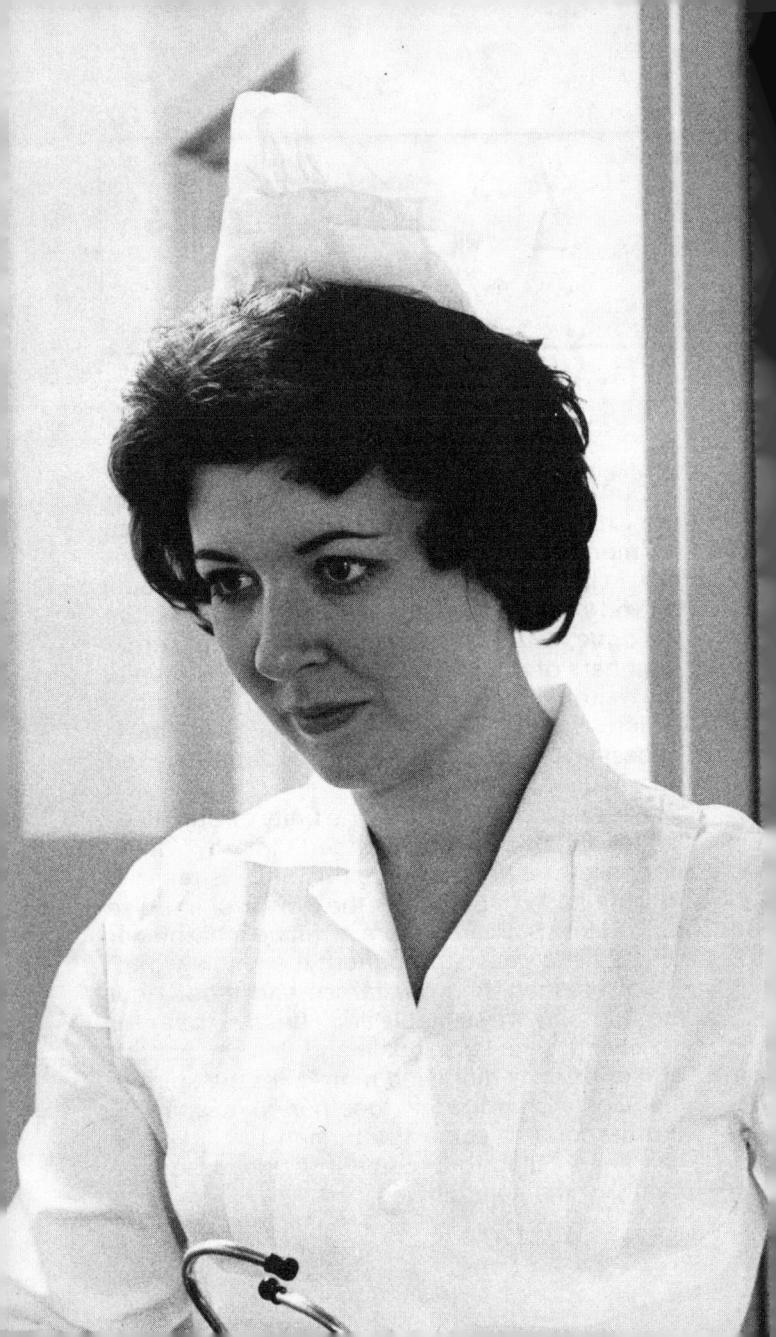

CHAPTER 2

Healer of Many Ills

"One day Jesus was teaching, and the power of the Lord made him heal. . ." (Luke 5:17).

The message of this chapter is that everyone of us in some way needs to be healed, and each one of us has healing power which too often we fail to make use of.

This is an insight which has come home to us in a special way in our time, and that is why I contend that in a spirituality for today every one of us must accept the responsibility of receiving and using the power of healing.

LIFE RESTORED

The word "healing" is understood here, of course, in a much broader connotation than the physical.

Physical ailments are surely within range of healing power. At Lourdes there is medical witness of dramatic cases of this kind. Less dramatic instances occur more or less frequently in all parts of the world, especially where groups of people are gathered in prayer.

But there are other areas of desperate need in the human condition: deep physical wounds which can and do respond to the healing touch of some person or a group of persons who are not afraid to invoke in prayer the gentle power of Christ.

Consider the parable of the Prodigal Son in St. Luke's Gospel, Chapter 15. There are three main characters in that parable. Two of them are healed, the third is not. There is much to be learned from the attitude of each.

The youngest son, coming home after his unhappy experience in a foreign land, having squandered his inheritance, bruised and bitter at life, is healed through his own sorrow and through the gentle forgiveness of his father.

The father, anxious and wounded by the precipitous departure of his son, is healed by the forgiveness that he generously extends to his chastened and repentant son. "He ran out to meet him, threw his arms around his neck, and kissed him" (Luke 15:20). "The father said to his servants: '. . . Let us eat and celebrate because this son of mine was dead and has come back to life. He was lost and is found'" (Luke 15:22-24).

But the one in this story who needs healing most of all is the one who adamantly refuses it. The eldest son grows angry at the gentleness of his father, and will not join the joyful guests. Eaten up by envy, blind to pity, and deaf to the pleading words of his father, how great is his need of the kind of healing that would soften his heart and allow room there for kindness and mercy. But the opportunity is lost because "the son grew angry at this and would not go in" (Luke 15:28).

This attitude of the elder son illustrates for us an important truth: Anger and bitterness and cynicism can effectively block off the healing process and even be the cause of new wounds on the human spirit.

After healing the sick who were brought to him, Christ told his apostles that they would be able to do even greater things than these. We need to ask ourselves whether, through our lack of faith, our fearfulness, our envy, our self-pitying bitterness, we have kept the power that Christ promised us too carefully hoarded within our narrow hearts.

INNER AND OUTER HEALING

Public healing has become a rather common phenomenon on the American scene. Oral Roberts, the late Katherine Kuhlman, and others have been able to fill auditoriums across the land and to reach millions through TV with their healing services.

The flamboyance of some of these spectacles may not be to our taste. And we may be inclined to question whether some of the cures are as genuine or lasting as they are made to appear. Dr. William Nolan, in a recent book entitled *Healing,* offered evidence on the basis of his personal research into specific cases of alleged healing by Katherine Kuhlman that six months later it was clear no permanent cures had taken place.

Worse than that, in the cases of two so-called faith healers, he found evidence of outright fraud and cruel deceit of those who had come in their desperation seeking help.

What this points out is the need of good judgment and discernment. But such misuse of human trust should not turn us aside from the reality that healing was an important part of Christ's pastoral concern, and remains an important concern of God's providence 2,000 years after Christ.

To concentrate on physical healing alone is a mistake. Healing of the spirit may well be even more significant. Doctors are more and more inclined to see the close connection between these areas of concern.

Dr. Karen Horney gives it as her considered opinion, after many years of psychiatric practice, that 85 percent of our population is neurotic, and one out of four of these is so seriously neurotic as to be in need of professional help.

All of these individuals have unsatisfied needs. They cannot express emotion, or cannot receive the expression of emotion by others, with the result that anxieties and phobias flourish in their lives. And physical ailments follow closely upon their emotional distress.

It is a matter of common observation, for example, that high blood pressure follows upon a condition of great psychic tension, as found in the type of person who is a perfectionist, a driver of himself and others, one who cannot be at peace with the element of chaos, the "unfinishedness," that enters into every human life.

CHARISMATIC HEALING

In the burgeoning charismatic movement healing has a special place, and it was here that

Father Francis MacNutt discovered his healing ministry.

As his interest in charismatic prayer grew, he met others who were well known for their special healing powers. He consulted and prayed with them, and found a healing power within himself.

Now he is called upon to lecture and to lead healing power sessions far beyond his St. Louis home base — not only in the United States but in Latin America and Australia. He has written two books on the subject, *Healing* and *The Power to Heal.* He states flatly: "I have seen many people healed, especially when I have prayed with a team or in a loving community."

In the Gospel accounts, Christ stands forth as the great healer of all ills. Are we justified in contending, Father MacNutt asks, that he does not have the same loving concern for those who are sick in body or mind or spirit today?

And he notes that the early Church acted as Christ did: The apostles proclaimed the Gospel and healed the sick. The New Testament letter of James, traditionally used as a scriptural foundation for the anointing of the sick, moves back and forth between forgiveness of sins and physical healing with no discernible change of assurance or emphasis:

"Is there anyone sick among you? He should ask for the presbyters of the church. They in turn are to pray over him, anointing him with oil in the Name (of the Lord.) This prayer uttered in faith will reclaim the one who is ill, and the Lord will restore him to health. If he has committed any sins, forgiveness will be his" (James 5: 14-15).

Father MacNutt feels that we have allowed our prejudices and inhibitions to block the healing power that otherwise might still be manifest among us, "whether we have sinned and need forgiveness, or are sick and need physical healing."

NEED FOR HEALING

Different kinds of sickness are in need of healing.

There is a sickness of the spirit caused by personal sin. Selfishness, stubbornness, pride, and the deliberate acts of malice they produce, cause a hardening, freezing effect on the soul.

In Dante's great epic poem, the *Inferno,* there is a graphic illustration of this truth. Led by the poet Virgil, Dante makes his way through the various levels of hell, noting that the punishment reserved for each person confined there is singularly suited to the nature of the crime committed.

But then he is led down to the very lowest depth of hell, where he sees Lucifer, the prince of that place of torment. The traditional way of portraying hell is as a place of fire, and one might suppose that Lucifer would be confined to the spot in hell where the fire was most intense. But this is where the genius of the poet manifests itself in a wonderful way. At the lowest part of hell, Dante sees a huge lake of ice, and in the center of that lake Lucifer is caught fast in that ice forever.

To be frozen in selfishness and pride is a terrible thing. But there is a warmth of healing that can melt the ice.

First of all, the ice is melted by warm tears of sorrow, and in that warmth the love of God can begin to grow. And often before there can be healing of some bodily ailment, this kind of healing of the soul must take place. When the paralytic was let down through the roof to the feet of Christ, Christ's first compassionate words were: "My son, your sins are forgiven" (Mark 2:5). Looking into this man's eyes, he saw the "humble and contrite heart" that brought forgiveness to King David after his crimes. Only then, as a kind of afterthought, Christ added:

"That you may know that the Son of Man has authority on earth to forgive sins . . . I command you: Stand up! Pick up your mat and go home" (Mark 2:10-11).

It should be added, of course, that Christ made provision for a sacrament of reconciliation in which this kind of healing of the selfishness of sin could take place, when joined to the true sorrow of the penitent. Perhaps we need a new recognition and use of this sacrament which in this time of change has come into a certain neglect.

The one who sins can heal himself by true sorrow, but there may well be needed the healing touch of someone else's hand to bring him to the point of repentance. Surely there is no greater gift of healing than by gentleness and sympathy and understanding to welcome the sinner home, as the father welcomed the prodigal son in our Lord's parable.

PSYCHIC HURTS

Emotional sickness also is common in the human condition, taking the forms of anxiety, melancholy, bitterness, cynicism.

More often than not this is caused by hurts nursed in the memory or even in the unconscious. Like a thorn festering in the finger or a small sharp stone in one's shoe, this kind of sickness is a constant source of irritation and pain.

It may have been caused by a misunderstanding between friends, or a slight — whether real or imagined — and the latter, perhaps, more often than the former. An unresolved argument may be its source or a lack of appreciation for some favor performed. Perhaps preference was given to someone else, and the thought of this rankles. Or it may well have been caused by such a downright lack of charity or injustice on the part of someone else that it seems impossible to forget.

How can this sickness be healed?

It is true to say that here the victim must be his or her own doctor, applying a salve of forgiveness. Through the application of this salve there can take place the healing of memories. This is a phrase often used by charismatics, and it has a real meaning and significance for all.

In our memories we store up too many recollections of slights or injuries that we have received, or that we imagine ourselves receiving. The healing process may be a painful one, but it is one that must be undertaken if we want to call ourselves genuine followers of Christ.

Christ left no doubt about his will in this matter:

"If you do not forgive others, neither will your Father forgive you" (Matthew 6:15). And he taught his followers to make this their frequent prayer:

Forgive us our sins
for we too forgive all who do us
　　wrong . . . (Luke 11:4).

In some quiet moment, when you are alone,
think of the person who offended you, perhaps
long ago, standing before you. Imagine yourself
looking directly at that person as you say: "I
forgive you as I hope to be forgiven by Christ." If
the thorn of resentment has dug deep, this may
be as painful as lancing the infected spot. But
quiet healing will follow.

The sign of peace, that we are asked to give at
Mass, is a symbolic gesture to indicate that we
want to extend our healing forgiveness to others
and are willing to accept the healing that others
are willing to apply to our faults.

Some people find difficulty with this custom,
raising the objection that it is only a surface
expression of peace. But it can have a deeper
meaning, if we so intend it. It can be symbolic of
the real desire on our part to forgive others as
Christ forgave his enemies. And how appropriate
it is at Mass, when we are about to receive the
Body and Blood of Christ, to extend forgiveness
in his name to the person next to us, who
represents all those with whom we come in daily
contact.

Doctors tell us that up to 80 percent of physical
ailments are psychic in their origin. If the distress,
the tension within the spirit, can be reached and
touched, often this will result in a restoration of
health to the body as well.

Father MacNutt states flatly that he has seen
physical healings follow upon release of inner
tension in prayer groups he has attended, most

often on retreats, when there is time for protracted prayer.

To have a special gift for releasing tension is not necessarily restricted to Christians; an ability of this kind can exist even in the natural order. Most of us have met or heard of individuals who by their gentle touch could bring about a certain release from pain.

Nevertheless, Father MacNutt thinks it wise to add this caution:

"A Christian has no business confusing Christian healing with any healing coming from spiritualistic sources. I think the wisest course is for us to learn to experience the beauty and power of Christian healing, to abstain from, while not condemning, any form of healing prayers that are not Christian, while clearly warning people to stay away from any healing connected with spiritualism and witchcraft."

Why is this warning in order?

Because there are evil spirits; and spiritualism, without making distinctions, too readily opens the door for their entrance. And because witchcraft sets up its own false god who may for a time simulate truth and goodness, but in the end engenders lies and hate and discord.

HEALING STARTS AT HOME

"When Jesus saw their faith, he said to the paralyzed man, 'My son, your sins are forgiven' " (Mark 2:5).

When we read the story of this paralytic, whom friends lowered through the hole in the roof to the feet of Christ, letting him down slowly on the swaying ropes, we should realize a little more clearly our own need of healing. And what this incident tells us is that we must be concerned with inner healing before we ask for physical healing, for that is the order in which Christ himself proceded.

We need to be healed of:

our unforgiving attitude;

our tendency to nurse small grudges;

our selfish concern with our own comfort;

our negativism, always seeing the worst side;

our quickness to criticize and belittle others;

our self-righteousness.

We surely need this kind of healing, and God is anxious to grant it to us, but only if we open up our minds and hearts to his coming, and cooperate with the Spirit who comes with him to stir us up in the search for truth.

Christ reaches out to us. The question is: How do we respond?

Responsibility is an important part of life. But just as important, and perhaps much more neglected, is a different way of putting it: response-ability.

How do we respond to the Spirit moving us to forgive ourselves and to forgive others without reservation?

How do we respond to the needs of those around us for the healing touch that we alone may be able to provide: our sympathy, our understanding, our prayer that goes beyond the formal and the ritual and reaches out to the bruised heart? How often have we been tongue-tied, caught up in an awkward silence, when a sick friend was longing silently to hear our healing expression of concern?

We have, many of us, lost that power of healing through nonuse, but it can be restored through our unselfish asking of the Christ, the great Healer.

And if we begin with that kind of healing, we can hope for other kinds of healing too, as Christ himself healed the paralytic and made him walk, but only after he forgave his sins.

Three Minute Meditation

Punishment That Brings Peace

Who would believe what we have
    heard?
  To whom has the arm of the Lord
  been revealed?
Yet it was our infirmities that he
    bore,
  our sufferings that he endured,
While we thought of him as stricken,
  as one smitten by God and afflicted.
But he was pierced for our offenses,
  crushed for our sins,
Upon him was the chastisement that
    makes us whole,
  by his stripes we were healed.
We had all gone astray like sheep,
  each following his own way;

But the Lord laid upon him
  the guilt of us all.
Though he was harshly treated, he submitted
  and opened not his mouth;
Like a lamb led to the slaughter
  or a sheep before the shearers,
    he was silent and opened not his
      mouth.
[But the Lord was pleased
  to crush him in infirmity.]
If he gives his life as an offering for
    sin,
  he shall see his descendants in a long
    life,
and the will of the Lord shall be accomplished through him.

                      Isaiah 53:1, 4-7, 10

INTERLUDE:

Love Is Open, Love Is Holy

Greetings to you, Valentine,
Half-seen there in your
    third-century Roman mist
Of truth and legend;
One thing, nevertheless, being true:
Your faith in Christ tested and enduring
Under the executioner's bright flashing sword.

I will not ask, holy bishop,
The origin of your strange repute
As encourager of yesterday's lovesick youth
Exchanging lace-pointed sugary greetings
And heart-shaped boxes
Full of sticky bonbon delights.

Never mind all that:
There is your present, pleasant burden
    of intercession
For us whose love is so often tinseled,
Sometimes perverse,
So often shallow,
(Our humanness unchanged
    by the long centuries).
Help us to strip away
The artificiality which clogs and confuses
    our love.
Teach us to respect love's wholeness,
And to understand love's holiness.
Don't let us cheapen what Christ held so dear.

We are not asked,
As you were,
To die for the faith we love.

To live our sorely tried love with calm courage,
That is our need.
That is the world's need.

Offer your bishop's prayer for youth,
So apt to be impatient with tradition,
For whom the Valentine sentiment
Is a quaint reminder
  of lavender-scented yesterdays.
Yet they cry out without words for love,
  these youth;
Help us to give them love,
Help them to find love and recognize its face.

Look with pity on those of us
  in middle years and beyond,
Groping through the deadening days
  of routine,
Restive and annoyed under youth's
  eagerness to change.
Make us gentle in our judgment,
Less attached to our preconceived ideas
Of the way things ought to be.
Help our love to be open
  to what is new and different,
Open to the exuberance of youth,
Open to the wide sweeping range
  of Christ's command:
Love your neighbor as yourself!

Comfort the aged,
Trembling with cold and the coming shadows,
So that in reliving their long years,
They recall not the bitterness,
But only the loving days and hours.

Remind us, Valentine,
When sterile self-pity
Distills harsh loneliness in our hearts,
That love grows on giving
Rather than receiving.
Where there is no love,
Inspire us to put love
So that we may find Love,
and with Love, lasting peace.

CHAPTER 3
Hardy Pioneers

A spirituality suited to today calls for something like the pioneering spirit that drove our American ancestors, fearlessly, into every corner of this vast continent.

When they wanted to make their way west into unknown and dangerous country, a common mode of action came to be followed. A number of families joined together and traveled as a group in their wagons, in a venture of mutual support.

In their wagons they had as much of the baggage of their former life as they could carry with them. Perhaps it wasn't much, but it made them feel less alone on the long unmarked road. And when they arrived at their destination and finally settled on their own land, these familiar objects would give them a sense of being home.

They knew where their roots were, and did not forget them even after 2,000 miles of rough passage and stirring adventure. But they also had to leave behind many of their material possessions and travel in a kind of rough simplicity that stripped them of their softness and hardened their spirits in the presence of adversity.

For months and even years, their condition was that of pilgrims, constantly moving onward, open to new sights and sounds, adjusting to new conditions and circumstances, maintaining their trust in God and in each other, no matter how difficult the way, no matter what tragedy introduced itself into their wandering lives.

ANCIENT PIONEER

Today, in this world of disturbing change, we have need once more of this pioneering spirit.

Perhaps the supreme model of daring trust in the Lord is Abraham, our "father in the faith," as St. Paul called him, because "By faith Abraham obeyed when he was called, and went forth to the place he was to receive as a heritage; he went forth, moreover, not knowing where he was going" (Hebrews 11:8).

This great patriarch emerges from the dim mist of history 3,000 years ago as a towering pioneer. Living among his own people in the Far Eastern city of Haran, he heard the Lord's call:

"Go forth . . . from your father's house to a land that I will show you" (Genesis 12:1).

It took courage and confidence to make that long journey of a thousand miles, and not by jet plane or comfortable car, but on foot, with his wife Sarai and some other members of his family. And he was 75 years old and childless. What promise could the future hold for him?

Yet he obeyed the Lord, and was able to adjust and adapt to new ways. And what blessings his faith and confidence in God have brought to all of us who have come after him down the centuries.

I would like to discuss in this chapter three characteristics of that spirit which are especially necessary in this world of disturbing change: simplicity, self-discipline, and openness to change.

SIMPLICITY

Simplicity can be defined in this context as a virtue which gratefully uses in moderation the material aids and comforts which America, this land of plenty, offers us, but without being so attached to them that their deprivation would rob us of our peace of mind. More than that, it means deliberately choosing to do with less, so as to be more free in reaching out to others and to God with our love.

Simplicity is not synonymous with actual poverty. Some who are poor in fact are far from simple in their envious desires. But it certainly implies a spirit of poverty and an uneasiness when we are reminded that some of our brothers and sisters in the human family are in dire want.

The conscience of a rich man must indeed be atrophied if he does not feel at least a little nervous at coming across Christ's statement about the rich man having the same difficulty in getting into heaven as a camel passing through the eye of a needle. Granted, we need not interpret that simile literally, but even taken figuratively it carries a somber note of foreboding.

The desire for a simple life flows naturally from the sympathy we are bound to feel for our brothers and sisters in the human family who live in actual and, sometimes, stark poverty: the 20 million families in the United States whose income is below the poverty level; the hundreds of millions of people in Third World countries for whom poverty means hunger, lack of proper shelter, early death.

Many young people today are providing us with an example of simplicity and a truly sympathetic heart. They show an ability to give and receive without grasping anything as their own. They gladly use material goods, but give the impression of not being too attached to them and that they could be happy even if deprived of them. Some of them have readily and cheerfully volunteered for service among the poor, sharing themselves fully with those in need.

POVERELLO

St. Francis of Assisi is the classic model of this kind of simplicity. No one enjoyed the beauty of God's world more than he did; and yet no one was more detached from the world. One of his biographers uses the expression "passionate detachment," as describing the thrust of his life once he had left his comfortable home and taken as his spouse "lady poverty," possessing nothing but the beggar's clothing he wore.

Nature lovers have always rightly regarded St. Francis as a special patron, and so should all who have an eye and a heart for the beauty of God's creation. St. Francis loved the world, and yet did not for a moment feel that he owned it or could dare to abuse it. He wanted to own nothing in the world; and yet with every step he took, his heart was consciously lifted up to God in gratitude for the gift of beauty which was his to enjoy. Thus he could sing:

Praise and bless the Lord,
    all his creatures!
Give thanks and serve him
    with great humility.

St. Francis would have smiled in approval of something Mother Teresa of Calcutta frequently says: "The poor are God's greatest gift to the world."

Perhaps we show that our mind set is different than that of Francis in a simple little phrase we use quite often: "I'm going to take a shower," or "take a walk in the woods," or "I'm going to take dinner." The implication in that word "take" is that the food or the beauty or the water is mine, and I intend to use it as my property.

Suppose I were to say: "I am going to give myself to the beauty of the woods," or humbly ask the service of "sister water," or, like a poor man, gratefully accept my food as a gift. What a different kind of approach this would be, and how it would open me to full enjoyment.

For there seems to be a law in nature: The more we try to possess the beauty of the created world selfishly, and claim it as exclusively our own, and hug it to ourselves so that nobody can share it, the more the wonder and freshness of that beauty slips through our fingers like water. Could that be why it seems to be a common phenomenon that prosperous celebrities and millionaires tour the world in search of new sensations, and at the end confess: Life is a bore!

Thinking about St. Francis and his simplicity, we might be a little less inclined to complain about the fact that we cannot afford all the comforts and luxuries that we would like to have. And this might make us a little more thoughtful of others who are hungry and cold and deprived of even the necessities of life. A spirituality that does not possess this kind of concern is threadbare in the world of want and suffering we live in.

SELF-DISCIPLINE

Self-discipline is not a popular concept today. Most of us take the comforts of life for granted, and are likely to complain if even our luxuries are tampered with.

But self-discipline is a necessary characteristic of the pioneering spirituality that is suited to today.

Self-discipline, of course, is the natural companion of simplicity, reflected so beautifully in the life of Francis of Assisi. A Franciscan writer, James Meyer, gave this virtue a practical setting for all who would like to walk in the Franciscan spirit:
1. No sin in heart or hand for the sake of goods or fortune;
2. Moderation in enjoying and acquiring goods or fortune;
3. Sharing goods or fortune with God and neighbor.

To follow that kind of program today is to be a pioneer, if one measures it against the spirit of the world. *Whatever Became of Sin?* is the title of a recent book by Dr. Carl Menninger, and his response to the question is that in the last 50 years sin disappeared somewhere along the line in the professional and popular view. He is convinced as a psychiatrist that it is time to reassert human responsibility in moral choices, as a factor of importance in understanding the human condition.

An authentic spirituality for today starts with the acceptance of responsibility for obeying God's law as expressed in its primitive form in the Ten Commandments. That is the most basic form of self-discipline that must be part of our lives.

For as God spoke to his people and to all of us through Moses:

"For this command which I enjoin on you today is not too mysterious and remote for you. It is not up in the sky, that you should say, 'Who will go up in the sky to get it for us and tell us of it, that we may carry it out?' Nor is it across the sea, that you should say, 'Who will cross the sea to get it for us and tell us of it, that we may carry it out?' No, it is something very near to you, already in your mouths and in your hearts; you have only to carry it out" (Deuteronomy 30:11-14).

Only if we blind ourselves can we be unaware of God's commands.

First comes the self-imposed blindness. Then the demon of permissiveness enters the heart through an unguarded door, whispering with pretended loving concern: "Do as everyone else does. Follow the impulse of the moment. Ethical principles are relics of the past. Put them out of your mind. Love of God and neighbor are totally unrealistic concepts for this time and place. You deserve all the pleasure you can squeeze out of life. Don't let anything or anyone stand in your way."

In such a selfish climate, spirituality, obviously, cannot thrive or even live. It needs the support of self-discipline, of self-imposed moderation, just as the pioneers in their wagon trains had to accept the wagon master's authority, divide equally the sometimes sparse rations, and live according to the laws that were necessary for survival itself in that rough terrain.

And survival itself depended on the mutual acceptance of discipline. No doubt, it happened in more than one wagon train expedition that a youthful member of the party grew impatient at the slow progress of the ponderous wagons and decided to strike out for himself, riding on ahead at top speed. But seldom if ever did such an attempt succeed. The distance and the hazards were too great. Either the lone traveler fell prey to the Indians, resentful of the intruders on their land, or else he died of thirst somewhere along the trail and left his bones to bleach on the desert floor.

HUMAN FRAILTY

It is no small exercise of self-discipline simply to accept the frailties of the human condition and to be patient with them.

St. Paul described this human need well, using another kind of simile:

"Athletes deny themselves all sorts of things. They do this to win a crown of leaves that withers, but we a crown that is imperishable . . . What I do is discipline my own body and master it, for fear that after having preached to others I myself should be rejected" (1 Corinthians 9:25, 27).

A pioneer must surely have a willingness to share, first of all, with his fellow pioneers in the journey to a God who sometimes seems distant. Their journey is such that all must depend greatly on the mutual support they can give to each other. But there must also be sharing with the multitude, bewildered, caught up in the false spirit of the times; sharing love and sympathetic understanding; sharing the light with all whose hearts are open to receive it.

This sharing spirit too is a very necessary characteristic of a spirituality suitable for today.

OPENNESS TO CHANGE

To be a pioneer is to experience a certain eagerness to explore the unknown, to venture out among the uncertainties and dangers of uncharted territory. And with this goes a willingness to adjust to rapidly changing circumstances, to events that were completely unanticipated.

Think once more of the people in the wagon train heading west, who every day had to be ready for the unexpected, and who reached their promised land only if they had the ability to adjust.

A spirituality suited to today needs that kind of adjustability. And alas! it seems to be the most difficult step for many to take.

Typical of human resistance to change is the story of the automobile. When the first self-propelled, steam-driven vehicle appeared in England in the early nineteenth century, hissing and snorting down the country roads, it caused much popular apprehension. As a result, a "red flag law" was passed in 1831, requiring that a horseless carriage of any kind had to be preceded by a man on foot carrying a red flag by day and a red lantern at night.

This red flag law remained in effect for 65 years; it was not repealed until 1896. Obviously, common sense dictated that it should have been repealed long before. But it remained on the books because a large number of people were determined to fight change in the manner of transportation, even when it was inevitable.

It seems obvious that the course of history has brought us to another era in which rapid change is taking place in the world, not only in the religious sphere but in every department of life. It is a different kind of world, and we have to adjust our thinking and change some of our modes of procedure in order to respond to it.

But for many people, change (whatever form it takes) is a threat and must be resisted at all costs. They favor their own special kind of "red flag law" to preserve the status quo and effectively block renewal and reform.

There is nothing new about this, of course. The prophet Jonah in the Old Testament is a classic example of a man who was unable to adjust to God's change of plan.

Sent to the wicked city of Nineveh by the Lord, he joyfully and zealously shouted his message:

"Forty days more and Nineveh shall be destroyed" (Jonah 3:4).

But the people of Nineveh unexpectedly repented of their wrongdoing, and God relented and withheld the threatened disaster.

This greatly displeased Jonah, and he became angry.

What a typically human response to change in the predicted or established order of things.

We are told that the Lord reproached Jonah: "Have you reason to be angry?... should I not be concerned over Nineveh?" (Jonah 4:4,11)

A spirituality suited to today does not get angry with God because his providence has so arranged it that we find ourselves living in a time of great cultural change. It does not proceed on the assumption that God's providential plan necessarily coincides with our view of what that plan should be.

Someone said to Abraham Lincoln during the Civil War: "Surely God is on our side." To which Lincoln replied: "I am more concerned about whether we are on God's side."

To be a spiritual pioneer today is to wholeheartedly accept the process of renewal in the Church as reflected in Vatican II and subsequent declarations.

It is to accept patiently the painful process of trial and error by which, acting collegially, the People of God are trying to realize that renewal and make it come alive in their worship and in their daily lives.

It is to have a realistic view of the human condition as compounded of the elements it has always possessed: a little unselfishness joined to a great deal of self-serving; pettiness and meanness of spirit, but an occasional outbreak of nobility that makes the spirit soar.

It is to be open to the endless variety of God's loving ways with humankind and the wide range of our possible response. So be it!

Three Minute Meditation

Service of the Poor

Born poor, but of humble and respected folk,
I am particularly happy to die poor,
having distributed . . . in the service of the poor
and of the holy Church which nurtured me,
whatever came into my hands —
and it was very little —
during the years of my priesthood and episcopate.
Appearances of wealth have frequently disguised
thorns of frustrating poverty
which prevented me from giving to others
as generously as I would have wished.
I thank God for this grace of poverty
to which I vowed fidelity in my youth,
poverty of spirit,
as a priest of the Sacred Heart,
and material poverty,
which has strengthened me in my resolve
never to ask for anything —
positions, money or favors —
either for myself
or for my relations and friends.

Pope John XXIII's *Journal of a Soul*

CHAPTER 4

Creators of Community

"One Christian is no Christian."

The quotation is from Charles Peguy, a French writer and precursor of renewal in the Church, who died along with millions of promising young men in the tragic holocaust of World War I.

Peguy also wrote: "When we get to heaven, God is going to ask us first: Where are the others?"

This was not, of course, a new concept. When the apostles quarreled about which of them deserved to be deputy commander in the army they thought Christ would raise, to drive the Romans out of their land and restore the glory of Israel, Christ quickly corrected them. Not self-glorification, but humble service of others is what he sought:

"Anyone among you who aspires to greatness must serve the rest, and whoever wants to rank first among you must serve the needs of all" (Matthew 20:26-27).

One of the insights of our day recognizes truth in these statements more clearly than Peguy's contemporaries saw it. He was a lonely prophet who found little acceptance in his time.

But what refreshing impulses to community love and service have developed in the modern spiritual climate!

In Cursillo and Marriage Encounter, in the growth of the charismatic movement, in the proliferation of shared prayer and Scripture sharing groups of various kinds, we have ample evidence of the fact that people are being drawn to warm and open expression of their dependence on each other, on their need for community.

Marriage Encounter is concerned with "making good marriages better." But the instinct and impulse of the movement is to bring other couples to a new awareness of sharing as instruments of love. Much wider is this need than that expressed in the selfish man's prayer:

God bless me and my wife,
My son John and his wife,
Us four,
No more.

THE WORLD BEYOND

If there was a time when the Church did not seem to be too concerned with reminding us of our duty to help solve the social problems of the larger human community, that time is past. Unmistakable is Pope Paul's view of the challenge in his encyclical letter, "Progress of Peoples," in which he is concerned with the economic imbalance between the "have nations" and the "have not nations" of the world:

"We want to be clearly understood on this point. The present state of affairs must be confronted boldly and its concomitant injustices must be challenged and overcome . . . Everyone must lend a ready hand to this task, particularly those who can do most by reason of their education, their office, or their authority."

And this thought was reinforced at the meeting of the World Synod of Bishops in 1971:

"Action on behalf of justice and participation in the transformation of the world fully appear to us as a constitutive dimension of the preaching of the Gospel, or, in other words, of the Church's mission for the redemption of the human race and its liberation from every oppressive situation."

A spirituality for today is sympathetic toward and accepts gratefully the concept that service of others, in small or large community, is essential if we are to keep growing toward the maturity it is possible for us to reach.

BRAVE NEW WORLD

In his novel *Brave New World*, Aldous Huxley chillingly describes, as he sees it coming, the loveless, scientific world of the future. There is community in that world, in the sense that people live in proximity to each other. But they live in identical cubicles; they are planned and programmed robots, nothing more. There is no growth of love and understanding. Each individual is unalterably fixed in his daily routine.

The family no longer exists in this bleak world, much less the Church. It becomes a crime against the State even to speak of such warm and human groupings.

We ought to think of that prospect when we get impatient, as we all do at times, with the failures and frustrations that are part of living in community, simply because to be human is to be capable of frailty and failure.

Consider the alternatives to our present imperfect condition:

The programmed world projected by some scientists appalls by its blindness to non-measurable human values, which are none the less real and enduring.

And at the other end of the spectrum we are also appalled (even while we are fascinated) by pessimistic novelists like Kurt Vonnegut and Peter DeVries, who seem to see life as ruled entirely by a blind and malignant fate. To accept that philosophy could only inspire us to a neurosis of desperation.

Built into a spirituality for today is the conviction that neither of these alternatives is acceptable or inevitable, and indeed both must be resisted with all our strength.

The programmed "brave new world" would do away with human freedom in the name of efficiency. Dictators throughout history have tried to establish that kind of world. But if they succeeded for a time, in the end they were defeated by the overwhelming rising up of their slaves answering to their God-given instinct to be free human beings.

Nor can a true believer in God as a God who supports but does not coerce his human family in the use of their freedom accept the pessimistic view that all is predestined by a cruel fate. "The fault," Shakespeare wrote, "lies not in our stars but in ourselves that we are underlings."

CHURCH: HUMAN AND DIVINE

There are many ways in which people create community. It is my conviction that the Church as community remains the chief providential instrument of our growth in spirituality and our ultimate salvation.

Within the Church there has been conflict, there has been human weakness, in every period of its history. Christ foresaw this when he founded the Church. But he knew also that something deep inside all of us cries out for the sharing and the shelter of a spiritual community; it is not good for anyone to be alone.

Some people are giving up on the Church today and for different reasons, but behind them all is an unwillingness to accept her human side.

Some say the Church has gone "liberal" and has abandoned too easily many of her venerable customs and traditions. Others profess to be alienated because the Church, they say, has been too slow to change, too ponderous in coming to grips with changed social conditions and problems. They find the Church too impersonal and legalistic in the handling of human problems.

There are different ways in which the word "Church" can be understood, and much confusion could be saved if this were kept in mind. There is the Church as instituted by Christ, with his promise that the gates of hell would not prevail against her. And there is the Church as represented by the persons who administer her affairs or who simply profess themselves to be her members.

If you are talking about Church in this second sense, it would be as untrue to say that the

Church has never blundered as it would be to say that the Church has always been heartless and unfeeling. It is precisely here that one must expect to see the human side, with all its range of possibilities — from nobility to selfish pettiness. Christ promised to preserve his Church to the end, but he did not give any guarantee against frailty and imperfection on the part of those in charge of practical affairs.

Freedom and intelligence are God's great gifts to his human creatures. He expects us to solve our problems by good judgment, and the fact is that we sometimes abuse our freedom and do not exercise good judgment. Why should anyone be surprised or scandalized at this?

"But the Church no longer answers our need for real community," some are saying, as they go out into the desert or the mountains to form new and idyllic communes. There they will again encounter all the faults and frailties of the human condition. But they must then meet them without the divine promise of guidance and the miraculous power of renewal, laborious and painful though it may be, that through the centuries have characterized the Church of Christ.

You will not find that remarkable power of renewal in Buddhism or Mohammedanism, other great religions, which remain through the centuries static and turned inward upon themselves.

Here are two ways in which renewal in the Church is finding expression in terms of building a strong community: in the collegial process and in the right use of power. A spirituality for today will be open to them and will make use of them, and will grow more mature in the very process of doing so.

COLLEGIAL PROCESS

"Collegiality" is a word widely used since Vatican II. That Council used it in explaining the relationship of the bishops with the pope as head of the Church. But in the intervening years it has come to be used in a much broader sense, as referring to the sharing of the decision-making process at all levels in the Church.

As a result, there has come about the proliferation of committees and councils, at the diocesan and parish levels, in religious communities, and in the international Synod of Bishops meeting at intervals in Rome.

It seems clear that the frustration level is rising in regard to the many meetings we are asked to participate in today, as new councils undergo their birth pangs and their tender infancy. Someone has said that meetings have become the official penance of the Church, taking the place of fast and abstinence.

Meetings can indeed be painful; they can be boring. They can be well-planned, but they can also be poorly planned. The people who attend them can be awkward, overbearing, poorly informed, hypersensitive, hung up on incidentals. They can also surprise by their dedication and their expertise.

But an alive and alert spirituality will not allow itself to be turned aside, by discouragement and frustration, from the reality that the Church, and the Holy Spirit acting in the Church, is asking all of us to move confidently in this direction. She is asking us to use the collegial approach as the preferred means of reaching a decision in any matter that affects the welfare of the community. Authority remains a reality, but the process of arriving at the moment when it is to be exercised is being reshaped.

Authoritarian procedures in reaching decisions were suited to another age, but for the Church to continue to use them now would be to deprive herself of credibility in this age. It will take time to perfect the new system of sharing responsibility, which we have timorously embarked upon; and it cannot be expected that this system or any other system, new or old, will work miracles.

Many of the less desirable aspects of the Roman style of lawmaking and law enforcing, in the past, found their way into the Church. Many of the less desirable features of democracy will also be visible in the new approach. The collegial approach will have to be transformed by the spirit of the Gospel if it is to serve the kingdom of God.

It is surely apparent that only a deep and sound spirituality will be open to the Spirit working among us in this new way.

Under a strong but not an arbitrary leader, it is not a hopeless ideal to reach consensus, understood not simply as a majority vote but a group decision arrived at after ample discussion. This happens in families and in business enterprises. It was such a consensus, arising out of countless meetings, that brought about the abolishing of the hideous practice of child labor in factories; here was a classic case of a consensus being translated into power.

RIGHT USE OF POWER

Our traditional asceticism mistrusted power, defined in the sense of bringing political influence to bear on existing social problems. It was an insight not given even to the great saints that they possessed power of this kind and should use it to remedy social injustice.

St. Alphonsus Liguori, founder of the Redemptorists, is a good example in point. Born of a well-to-do family in Naples, Italy, he turned his back on the success he had begun to achieve, first as a lawyer, then as a priest who seemed marked for higher station, and went into the mountain villages to work unselfishly for simple uneducated people he found there. It became his lifework to instruct them in their faith and preach to them about the love of God. And he founded the Redemptorist Congregation of priests in the first instance to carry on this apostolate.

But he was not inspired to make an effort, on the social level, to change laws which were unjust or to promote social legislation which would relieve their grinding poverty. And it was a very real poverty. There were a small number of the rich, and a great mass of the desperately poor. Something of the same condition of imbalance can be seen in Third World nations today.

The eighteenth century in Italy was, of course, a very different world. Democracy was unknown; voting by the populace was unheard of. The democratic idea was struggling to find a concrete expression in America, the New World, just as Alphonsus was entering his extreme old age.

The fact that in those circumstances and in that place he lacked the insight and privilege that now we take for granted does not make him any the less a saint. Possessing that privilege simply gives us added responsibility. And I suggest that using that privilege as power, on behalf of justice and truth, is closely connected with our growth in spirituality.

Power is a threatening word, and carries with it the implication of browbeating and violence. Christ did not exercise this kind of power (except for one noteworthy time in the temple court against the moneychangers), so why should we? Obviously, browbeating others is not going to enhance their or our own spiritual growth.

But to use the power inherent in a group of people united in their devotion to a cause; to join with others in speaking out in a united way for basic human rights, including the right to life of the unborn, this kind of power the Church clearly urges us to use today. To prove this to yourself, if you are tempted to disbelieve it, you need only read two encyclical letters: "Peace on Earth" by Pope John XXIII and "Progress of Peoples" by Pope Paul VI.

PERSON-TO-PERSON

Jean Steinman in his thought-provoking little book, *Christian Faith for Today,* points out that we don't have faith in a thing or a system; we have faith in a person.

There is a sense, of course, in which we can speak rightly of "faith in the Church." But even here what we mean is faith in Christ, who founded the Church and by his presence makes it a living, breathing organism.

We need a structure to which we can relate and in which we can find support and guidance; and there must be laws and commonly cherished observances, or the structure will fall apart.

But a system of laws, a collection of observances, taken by themselves are dead, not alive. They participate in life only when living persons use them and live by them.

It is important to have a structure of laws, but it is more important to undertake the task of building a community of persons, based on respect and love for each other as persons. To build community in this way may be a slow and tedious task but the Spirit is calling us to that task in a special way in our time.

"This is proof of nobility of soul and generosity of spirit," St. John Chrysostom wrote, "to refuse to stand by and watch the afflictions of others, even if one has no mandate to relieve them."

Love of Christ, love of each other. If we do not have this kind of love, we do not deserve to survive as a believing community. If we do have it, there is no limit to our growth in spirituality. There is no limit to what we can accomplish for the building up of God's kingdom on earth.

I Am Here!

Here is a measure and a test of your growth in spirituality from a much venerated Old Testament prophetic book:
This, rather, is the fasting that I wish:
    releasing those bound unjustly,
    untying the thongs of the yoke;
Setting free the oppressed,
    breaking every yoke;
Sharing your bread with the hungry,
    sheltering the oppressed and the
        homeless;
Clothing the naked when you see them,
    and not turning your back on your
        own.
Then your light shall break forth like
        the dawn,
    and your wound shall quickly be
        healed;

Your vindication shall go before you,
  and the glory of the LORD shall be
    your rear guard.
Then you shall call, and the LORD will
    answer,
  you shall cry for help, and he will
    say: Here I am!
If you remove from your midst oppression,
  false accusation and malicious speech.

Isaiah 58:6-9

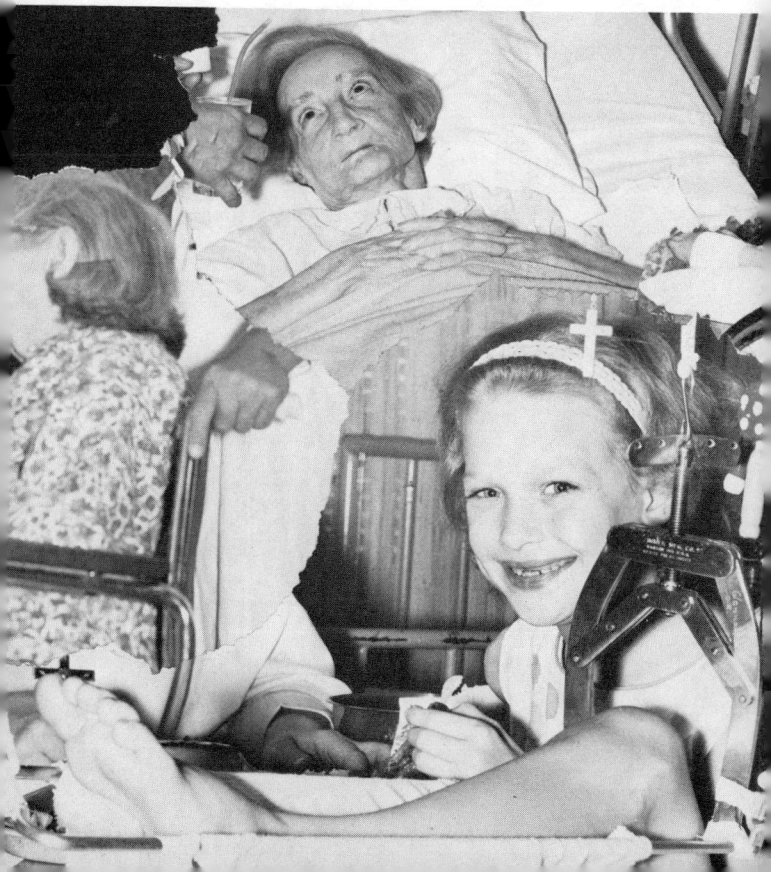

Warm - hearted Contemplatives

What happens when a star collapses?

"Implosion" is the comparatively new word astronomers use to describe this phenomenon, in which a star literally caves in on itself. Thus it is just the opposite of explosion, which connotes an outward blast, with fragments being violently hurled in all directions.

In implosion the elements of a star, at some late stage of its development, are dragged inexorably by unimaginable forces of gravity toward its center. The collapsed body is called a neutron star. It is so densely packed that if the earth were collapsed to the density of such a star it would be only about 300 feet in diameter.

In this same class of phenomena is the so-called dark hole, a collapsed star far out in the universe in which the force of gravity is so great that not even light can escápe; it can be detected only by the radioactivity it generates.

One of these implosions was recorded on giant radio telescopes in September 1972. The signal came from a point thousands of light years distant from our galaxy. Observers knew that an implosion had taken place because Cygnus X-3, as the mysterious phenomenon was called, suddenly generated a 200 percent increase in radioactivity.

What is my point? Simply this: If we want to be effective in reaching out to others with our healing love, we must first turn inward to the depths of our own hearts and encounter there, in a kind of spiritual implosion, the God who awaits us and invites us to regular and deep reflective prayer.

DEEPENING PROCESS

Thomas Merton, for 27 years a Trappist monk at Gethsemani Abbey in Kentucky, died, tragically, December 10, 1968, in Bangkok, Thailand, electrocuted by the faulty wiring in an electrical appliance. Through his writings he had become famous in his lifetime as a spiritual guide for the fretful world of the fifties and sixties. At the time he died, he was attending an international conference, at which Western and Oriental experts had gathered to discuss the modes of contemplation.

It was Merton's firm belief, repeated many times in his books, that the most pressing need to be found in the world today is for people in all walks of life to understand and put into practice the habit of reflective prayer. It is the only way, he wrote, to deepen our own self-understanding, freedom, integrity, and capacity to love. And without that deepening process, even though we are well-intentioned, we will not have anything of value to give to others or to the world. As Merton eloquently expressed it in *The Climate of Monastic Prayer:*

"We will communicate to them only the contagion of our own obsessions, our aggressiveness, our egocentric ambitions, our delusions about ends and means, our doctrinaire prejudices and ideas. We have more powers at our disposal today than we ever had, yet we are more alienated and estranged from the inner ground of meaning and love than we have ever been."

The phrase "contemplative prayer" no doubt has a strange ring for many. They associate it with monks or cloistered nuns, whose lives, they think, are hopelessly remote from the concerns of ordinary human life.

But if Merton was right, and his rightness is being convincingly reasserted by a large number of modern writers on spirituality, contemplative prayer must in some measure be the concern of everyone. There are degrees of involvement, of course, depending on temperament and circumstances. But every one of us is called, in some way, to walk an inward and solitary path to our unique meeting place with God.

MYSTERY IN SIMPLICITY

What awaits us at that inward meeting place?

The opportunity to simply be attentive, be aware, be awake to God. And in responding to that opportunity, we witness to the mystery of divine aloneness, that of God in himself and of each one of us within God, beyond any sign or thought or word.

When God spoke to Moses in the burning bush, Moses approached in reverence and awe and said: "Who are you?"

But God would not give the kind of answer Moses sought. God did not respond: "I am the omnipotent all seeing Creator of the universe, and I will now let you see what I look like, so that you can describe me to the people you are sent to save."

All that God would say to Moses was: "I am who am" (Ex 3:14). It was as if he had said: "I am light in darkness. I am mystery in simplicity. You can never know me, yet you must never cease striving to know me. I am that which cannot be described in human words, yet I am the Word."

It is very significant that God would not describe himself in the concrete terms that Moses desired. Moses had to be content, and we must be content, with a mysterious God beyond human understanding, yet also a God who loves us and invites us to approach him along the path of the mystic. We cannot see his face, but we can be increasingly certain of his presence.

MODERN MYSTICS

It is time indeed to bring the word "mystic" back into good repute. Tabloid journalism, always on the lookout for the sensational, has given a bad name to mysticism. The misconception has grown that from it one must expect strange and weird phenomena. False visionaries appear on the scene, flourish for a time, and gather their following. Then, alas, it becomes clear that they were victims of hysteria or exhibitionism. For some people the generalization quickly follows that all "mystics" are self-deluded or fraudulent.

But there are, and there have always been, genuine mystics on the human scene. Two of the greatest of them, St. Teresa of Avila and St. John of the Cross, lived and died in Spain in the sixteenth century. Their books offer a kind of road map of contemplative prayer and the various deepening levels at which it can be practiced. St. Teresa herself sounded the mystical depths, and left a vigorous and vibrant record of what she thought and felt about the experience, in her *Autobiography* and the *Interior Castle.*

Yet no one was more suspicious of "mystic phenomena" than these two great mystics. Their works are studded with warnings against our being taken in by such phenomena, as if they were the desirable goals of prayer. Strange things happened to Teresa in her prayer, and her nuns were startled at them, but she never ceased to plead with God that her prayer, at least in its outward appearance, would be simple and ordinary.

A modern writer, Father Andrew Greeley, in his book *Ecstasy, a Way of Knowing,* contends that an occasional mystical experience (call it ecstasy) is not at all uncommon and that millions of people, perhaps half the population, in our society have this kind of experience and in a variety of settings: listening to music, childbirth, the beauty of a quiet sunset. And surely we must add the setting of deep reflective prayer.

Greeley reaches the same conclusion as St. John of the Cross and St. Teresa: While remaining open to its possibility, "one ought to be extremely skeptical and cautious about the direct pursuit of ecstasy." There is too much danger of delusion along that path.

But guarding against delusion should not mean giving up contemplative prayer. That would be to foster still another delusion — that life lived entirely on the surface can bring us any genuine happiness or peace.

There is no more dangerous delusion than the one fostered by the saying one hears quite often: "My work is my prayer." The implication, of course, is that quiet and reflective prayer is unnecessary in our busy lives. To act on that assumption is to guarantee that our work will have a very shallow foundation and that we will communicate to others, as Merton put it, only our prejudices, delusions, and obsessions.

CIRCLES OF CONTEMPLATION

How can we love and pray to a God we can't see? We can catch glimpses of God at three different levels in life, in three concentric circles.

World of Nature

God can be glimpsed in the created beauty that he has placed around us in his world. What is needed on our part is the conscious recognition of his presence.

The emphasis here should be on the word conscious.

We have all experienced the expectant joy of an early sunrise, the song without words of a wheat field stirred by the wind, the heart-lifting sight of geese flying north in perfect formation, the peaceful stillness of a summer evening.

But how often have we consciously reminded ourselves that the joy, the gladness, the peace could not be in these sights unless they were first present in God, whose creative energy made them come to pass? How many of us, recollecting some heart-lifting moment, would be able to say that we had consciously recognized and rejoiced in God's presence?

But these moments pass so quickly. If we do not notice them they are lost forever. There is something in our human condition that longs for that kind of awareness, and that is why St. Francis of Assisi is so universally known and loved. We envy, even while we rejoice in his intimacy with all of God's creatures, great and small. There was a simplicity about his attitude, referred to in another chapter as an important characteristic of a spirituality suited to today. But the simplicity stemmed from his clear-sighted vision of God in all the beauty of God's world.

To develop that same clear-sighted vision is the first stage on our journey toward a genuine contemplative orientation in our lives.

Other People

In a second and inner concentric circle stand all of our brothers and sisters in Christ, who said: "I assure you, as often as you did it for one of my least brothers, you did it for me" (Matthew 25:40). If we complain that we cannot see God, is it because we fail to look for him in the place where he himself said he would be?

Once more, consider St. Francis of Assisi.

Seeing God so vividly in the beauty of God's creatures all around him, he naturally responded in a loving way to the presence of God in every person whom he met.

One day he encountered on the road a most miserable leper with sores. Overcoming his initial feeling of disgust, Francis embraced and kissed him, and saw clearly, in a moment's vision, that he had performed this act of charity for Christ.

In Rome, Francis, a threadbare beggar, walked in upon Pope Innocent and the dignitaries gathered around him in the overblown Renaissance splendor of the Vatican court. Yet over this wide gulf Francis looked with love into the eyes of the pope and won his complete trust.

And there were others: simple Brother Juniper, who followed Francis like a faithful dog, and St. Clare, rich and noble, who learned from Francis what it really meant to love God, and dedicated her life to that love in the cloister.

What was the secret of Francis' attraction to these and so many other varied types? Surely it was because he saw Christ in each of them, and affirmed the worth of each of them as a carrier of Christ. Thus, with every human contact he deepened his awareness of God's presence in the world. The more people he met, the more of a contemplative he became.

And thus he showed us how to pull aside another veil that hides us from the face of God.

Our Own Souls

And now we come to the innermost concentric circle, where God is waiting to show us his face.

"Whenever you pray," Christ told us, "go to your room, close your door, and pray to your Father . . ." (Matthew 6:6).

That secret place within each one of us is where our uniqueness resides. God has something special to say to each of us in that secret place that he will not say to anyone else in the world. There, also, each of us has the capability of saying a special word to God that no one else can say.

But our problem is that we too often lack the patience to wait for God to speak, or to distill and draw from our heart's depth the answer it is in our power to give.

Each of us is called to a spiritual Helen Keller experience, overcoming our blindness and deafness, breaking through the barriers of darkness and silence.

Helen Keller had to learn, painfully, how to communicate with the outside world. Our task, in the midst of material cares, is to learn the foreign language of communication with the mysterious God who is within our souls. Helen Keller had her devoted companion, Anna Sullivan, to clear the way. And providence sends guides for us also, if we are willing to look for them, to accept their help in breaking through the tangible and sensate and material world that surrounds us, to learn the language that is beyond earthbound sounds and sight.

But there is no substitute for the initial and continuing effort to learn how to live and be at peace in the desert and the darkness of contemplation, where God awaits us as a friend.

The setting for this kind of contemplative prayer can be any place where there is quiet, where we can be alone. It can be in a church, the woods, a boat, an easy chair — even a bathtub, as Father Bernard Basset suggests with a smile in one of his popular and perceptive books on spirituality. The reason he offers is that the bathtub has some of the contours of a coffin, and so lends itself to solemn and sobering reflections on the shortness of life.

The right book as a starter for reflection is important: the kind of book written by the kind of person who has something special to say to us as unique individuals. There are books like that for every one of us, if we are patient in our search for them. Among them, surely, the Scriptures must have the place of honor as an essential contemplative tool, tried and tested through the centuries by saint and sinner alike. And the several new annotated translations offer a depth of understanding that previous generations did not have at hand.

"Comfortable, but not too comfortable" is the advice sometimes given when people ask: What is the best posture for reflective prayer? Whether we sit or stand or kneel is surely not of great concern to God, who is more interested in our prayer itself than the posture that we assume.

And yet there is something to be learned from the holy men of India and the Far East in this respect. They put some emphasis, and we should too, on such accompaniments to prayer as deep and regular breathing, an erect back, and a disciplining of the body to quiet relaxation.

AUGUSTINE'S INSIGHT

St. Augustine wrote glowingly of the "beauty ever ancient, ever new" that had captivated his heart and had at certain moments in his life lifted him into a state of ecstatic joy.

One of these moments he captured for us in glowing words that after all the centuries have never lost their power to warm the reader's heart.

The place was Ostia, seaport of Rome. The time was shortly after Augustine's conversion in Ostia, so longed for and prayed for by his mother, Monica.

Having decided to return to Africa, their homeland, they were resting in Ostia in preparation for the arduous sea journey. Mother and son stood together at a window which looked inward to the garden of the house where they were staying. Fifteen years later Augustine described the scene in these words:

"And our conversation had brought us to this point, that any pleasure whatsoever of the bodily senses, in any brightness of corporeal light, seemed to us not worthy of comparison with the pleasure of that eternal light, not worthy even of mention. Rising as our love flamed upward toward that Selfsame, we passed in review the various levels of bodily things, up to the heavens themselves, whence sun and moon and stars shine upon this earth.

"And higher still we soared, thinking in our minds and speaking and marveling at your works; and so we came to our own souls, and went beyond them to come at last to that region of richness unending, where you feed Israel forever with the food of truth and where life is that Wisdom by which all things are made; both the things that have been and the things that are yet to be . . . .

"And while we were thus talking of his Wisdom and panting for it, with all the effort of our heart we did for one instant attain to touch it; then sighing and leaving the first fruits of our spirit bound to it, we returned to the sound of our own tongue."

We who believe in Christ are called, as Augustine was, to reflect him to an unbelieving world. But to do this effectively, we must first find and learn to love him in the inmost center of our souls, in that dark light with which the brightest corporeal light is not worthy of comparison.

If we learn to contemplate Christ there; if we can accustom ourselves to see him in everyone who crosses our path in life; if we can consciously rejoice in his beauty, as St. Francis did, as we walk through the world he made, then our spirituality will truly be a source of peace and joy and a blessing to our brothers and sisters in Christ.

Light and Melody

What is it that I love, my God, when I love You?
Not the beauty of any bodily thing,
nor the order of the seasons,
not the brightness of light
that rejoices the eye,
nor the sweet melodies of all songs,
nor the sweet fragrance of flowers and spices,
not manna nor honey,
not the limbs that carnal love embraces.
None of these things do I love in loving my God.
Yet, in a sense, I do love light and melody,
fragrance and food and embrace
when I love my God:
the light and the voice and the fragrance,
and the food and embrace in the soul
when that light shines upon my soul
which no place can contain,

when that voice sounds
which no time can take from me.
I breathe that fragrance
which no wind scatters,
I eat the food
which is not lessened by eating,
and I lie in the embrace
which satiety never comes to sunder.
This it is that I love when I love my God.

Confessions of St. Augustine

INTERLUDE:

Mystical Reign in Spain

Doctor Teresa of Avila,
indomitable yet tender,
mystic respected by merchants,
I hail you across three centuries:
Founding your dozen convents in Castile,
bumping along in your antique carriage,
mothering timid young nuns in bare houses,
yet deeply at peace in that inmost room
of your own interior castle,
where the seraph pierced your heart
with the lance of love.
(Bernini captured the mystic moment.)

My prayer is poverty-stricken,
help me to enrich it.
My prayer-time is minimal,
let me learn from your firm gentleness
to enlarge it.
You said:
"God save me from sad saints!"
Show me how to be joyful at prayer,
how to make my prayer profound,
yet not pretentiously pious.

When your carriage overturned
on that rutted village road
and spilled you in the ditch,
you wryly said:
"If God treats his friends thus,
no wonder He has so few!"
You brought laughter to your prayer;
I need to learn your lightness.
I'm so heavy-handed when I speak to God,
impatient with his gentle silence,
weighted down with foolish inhibitions.

You could snap people quickly enough
out of their self-pitying melancholy.
To your nuns who suffered thus
you said briskly:
"Don't be selfish daydreamers.
Prayer is not a self-indulging time.
Don't let it be a narrow, introspective,
cramped, self-pitying kind of prayer.
Let it be generous, open-hearted,
joyful and forgiving.

And don't look for raptures and ecstasies;
delusion lies in ambush down that road."
You had raptures yourself, Teresa,
and an occasional ecstasy,
but they alarmed you
and you begged the Lord to banish them.

I see you behind your grille
consulting with Fray John of the Cross.
Your little Seneca, you called him,
so humble, wise, and so impractical,
(as a practical woman
you had to smile at his sackful of clocks)
exquisite poet, profoundly mystical,
bearing so patiently his own dark night,
and showing how Mount Carmel could be scaled.

Across the years your double witness stands:
The prayer of contemplation is for all.
God waits for every adventuresome soul
willing to seek him out in the silent desert
under the peaceful stars.
Teach me the way that you two learned so well,
the way my fretfulness has made me lose.
Teach me, Teresa; teach me, John,
what it really means to pray.

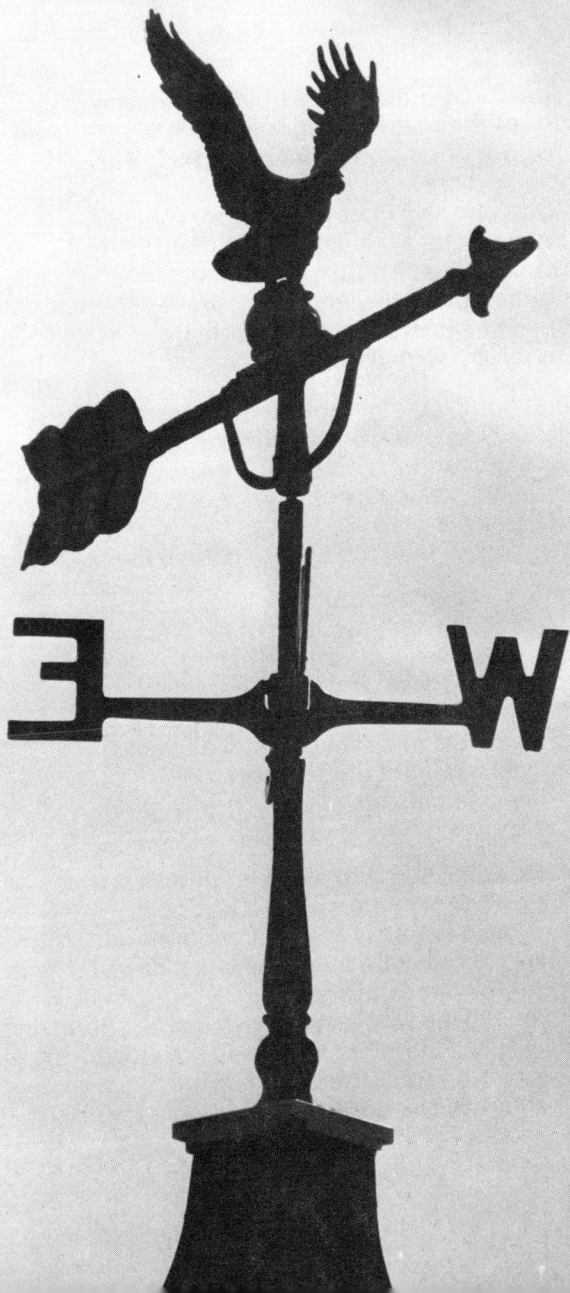

CHAPTER 6

Discerning Disciples

Augustine was 31 years old, and his world was crumbling.

This successful young teacher of rhetoric in Milan in the year 385 A.D. was convinced the Christian claims were true, and therefore he must be willing to offer his obedience to the Church and leave behind him the dark mysteries of the Manichees.

And yet he still shrank from the commitment to bring his passions under control and walk a path as straight as the Christian way of life would impose upon him.

Writing about this moment 15 years after his conversion, in his *Confessions* he described how, by the grace of Christ, he was inspired to seek counsel and direction:

"It came into my mind, and the idea appealed to me strongly, to go to Simplicianus, whom I knew to be your good servant, for your grace shone in him. I had heard that from his youth he had lived in great love of you. He was now grown old; and it seemed to me that from a long lifetime spent in so firm a following of your way he must have experienced much and learned much.

"And truly so it was. I hoped that if I conferred with him about my problems he might from that experience and learning show me the best way for one affected as I was to walk in your path."

There is no one who does not in some way share this need for counsel. A spirituality suited to these changing times must have a special recognition of this need.

Henri Nouwen in his book *Genesee Diary* quotes a French priest, a friend of his, who after 15 years of hearing confessions said he had reached two conclusions:

1. People aren't very happy,
2. We never grow up.

Think about that judgment for a moment, and ask yourself if it applies to you. And if it does, may it not be true because you have been closed in upon yourself, unwilling or afraid to trust yourself to someone who, taking an objective view, might be able to point out a vast but unused potential in your spiritual life?

Unfortunately, too many, it seems, fall into the category accurately described by Cardinal John Henry Newman:

"With regard to many good people, it is not so much that they want to please God, as they want to please themselves without displeasing God."

What will move you from this well-worn path of mediocrity?

MOVE TOWARD MATURITY

Spiritual direction can be an important instrument in accomplishing this, in the sense of using one of several means to gain an honest evaluation of your motives, your goals, your attitudes, your presuppositions, with a view to discovering and accepting your unique spiritual life direction.

These are the ideas of Father Adrian Van Kaam, one of the great living authorities on this subject and the author of many books out of the background of his "Institute of Man" at Duquesne University.

Through spiritual direction you can learn to keep all your duties in their proper perspective, giving the right priorities to the most important of them. Spiritual direction can open your eyes to opportunities you might not see with your own limited vision. As it enables you to grow in maturity, it enlarges your influence on the people you come into contact with, awakening them, as you yourself gradually awaken, to a fuller sense of truth and justice.

There is a kind of lavender-and-old-lace perfume about spiritual direction that needs to be dissipated. For priests and religious particularly, the phrase may carry with it a connotation of a somewhat formal and mechanical approach to the spiritual life, as reflected in some of the ascetical manuals of a past time.

But spiritual direction is coming into a new and better understanding today as being something that is always useful, and sometimes necessary, to continually open up to everyone the wider horizons of potential growth in Christ. You may have developed all kinds of psychological and sociocultural ways of refusing or concealing the call of the Holy Spirit in your life. A good spiritual director can help you penetrate through the mask that you hide behind, can make you conscious of the obstacles that you place in the way of the entire fulfillment of your personal potential to love and serve God.

It is not counseling that we are talking about here. Counseling is in its very nature problem-oriented. Spiritual direction is growth-oriented; it is concerned with personal adjustment to the present circumstances of your life with their potential for spiritual growth. It would surely be to miss out on an important instrument of help if one were to judge that this instrument could serve no useful purpose in one's life.

SIGNS OF THE TIMES

One of the few times recorded in the Gospels when it seems that Christ became angry is in a confrontation with the Pharisees and Sadducees. They asked him as a test to show them some sign in the sky that his mission was authentic. And Christ replied with a question: "If you know how to interpret the look of the sky, can you not read the signs of the times? An evil, faithless age is eager for a sign, but no sign will be given it except that of Jonah" (Matthew 16:3-4).

If some of those who lived in the time of Christ could blind themselves to the signs of his divine presence, there is surely danger that in our day we too might be blind to the signs of his immediate presence in the world. "I fear that Jesus might pass by," St. Augustine wrote, "and I might fail to recognize him."

Or if we see the signs, there is a danger that we may not read them right. Pope John spoke of the "signs of the times" in his opening address at Vatican II, and he made it clear that he did not want to be included among the prophets of doom, who read into the changes taking place in the world all sorts of disasters pending for the Church.

For him these were "omens portending a better day for the Church and for mankind."

Then in his landmark encyclical "Peace on Earth" he spelled out several of these omens, which we paraphrase as follows:

1. Ordinary people all over the world are increasingly seeking a share in the good things life is able to give them.

2. Women are becoming ever more conscious of their human dignity. They will not tolerate being treated as inanimate objects or mere instruments but claim, both in domestic and public life, the rights and duties that befit a human person.

3. In all nations and among all peoples there is a fading of the superiority complex which had its roots in socioeconomic privileges, sex, or political standing.

Put into popular phrases, these signs of the times come out as: minority uprisings, women's lib movement, and Third World revolution.

How do you relate to these phenomena of our day?

If they make you feel angry and threatened, perhaps this is a measure of your need for the kind of counsel that will help you to see things in a different perspective and restore peace to your troubled soul.

MOTIVE TO LEARN

Psychologists today use a phrase called "teachable moment" to describe the time when a person faces a task in a new situation demanding a quick response. At such a time one's motive to learn is intense, and the process of education can be very effectively accomplished.

Thus a young man might be told that he has a chance to advance in the corporation he works for, but it will mean taking over a new department. Because he is vitally interested, he will learn very quickly what he needs to know.

Sickness or death or the birth of new life or the moment of truly accepting Christ: These are important "teachable moments," when a good spiritual director can help you grow in the knowledge and love of Christ working actively in your life.

DYNAMIC DIRECTION

If you have a specific person in whom you have confidence, to whom you can go on a regular basis for direction, then you have much to thank God for. In this personalistic age, the need for this kind of person-to-person relationship is felt with special acuteness. Should you become conscious of this need at this point, it is important to set about searching for such a director — someone who can respond to this longing. It might be a lengthy search — and it might not succeed. There seems to be a great shortage of those who are willing and able to take on this task.

But if the search has been fruitless, you should not become discouraged. The Lord will be pleased by the search itself. Besides, God's providence has a way of intervening and sending the right kind of director in moments of crisis, even if only in a passing and a transient way.

Father Adrian Van Kaam feels that in our present circumstances it is unrealistic to expect that a personal, one-to-one spiritual director will be commonly available. Life is simply too various and complex to permit it, at least on a regular basis. So he saw the need for a do-it-yourself approach. This has led him to write a book which he has called *Dynamics of Spiritual Self Direction.* The chief instrument that he proposes as a substitute for a director is spiritual reading. This is admittedly another of those old-fashioned terms which is taking on new meaning today. Perhaps you are one of those who are turned off by the mere thought of spiritual reading. This is probably a legitimate reaction to some of the sugary lives of the saints and treatises on asceticism that prevailed on the scene for many years. Classic works on spirituality have always been available, of course, but in too many books there was a certain shallowness and unrealistic approach to life.

The newer books on prayer and the spiritual life — and a great many of them are appearing — reflect with fresh beauty the spirit of renewal that is breathing in the Church. Writers like George Maloney, Carlo Caretto, Morton Kelsey, Edward Farrell, and William Johnston, to name just a few, are offering insights on reflective prayer which are suited in a wonderful way to our felt needs. And Thomas Merton remains a perceptive and persuasive guide. His little book *Contemplative Prayer* is a classic of its kind.

To read and meditate upon wisely chosen books of this kind will certainly lessen the danger of becoming a victim of passing fads, the devotee of a facile psychologism, or the captive of small devotions blown out of proportion. Nor, of course, should such classic masters of the spiritual life as Thomas à Kempis, St. Francis de Sales, and St. Alphonsus Liguori be neglected. Above all, the Scriptures should provide an inexhaustible well of enlightenment and encouragement for spiritual growth.

It seems clear that if spiritual reading is to be effective it has to be serene, prayerful, and diligent. When you find writers that evoke a resonance in your own interior life, it is important to stay with the words that are able to touch you, words that are able, in a mysterious and grace-filled way, to bridge the gap and make their appeal to your uniqueness. What such writers are able to do is to open up to your view that hidden part of your being, that secret room at the very center of your being which only God can find and occupy. There is no way in which you can share this uniqueness with anyone else, not even with your marriage partner or your closest friend. To attempt to do so is to be unfulfilled and to be ill at ease and unhappy as a consequence. In the silence and secrecy of your uniqueness, God speaks to your soul words that are meant for your soul alone. You have special words to say to God that no one else can say in quite the same way.

People often complain of loneliness, but this may well be due to the fact that they are unwilling to understand and to accept the way they are meant to be: their lives completely open to God. St. Augustine expressed it poetically many years ago: "You have made us for yourself, oh God, and our hearts are restless until they rest in you."

As a practical suggestion, it is important to set aside a regular place and time for this kind of reflective reading. It should not be left to a vague general intention, but should be pinned down to a specific pattern and made a matter of regular routine. Nor should there be discouragement if not much seems to happen out there in the desert and if the mind produces nothing but distractions. To become contemplative means to be courageous, even when your prayer seems to be a dry and dusty journey into darkness. But in that darkness, patiently waiting, is Christ, ever eager to become your Way, your Truth, and your Life.

GROUP DIRECTION

While it is true that a certain part of you is so unique that it can be shared only with God, it is also true that much benefit can come by belonging to a group that is dedicated to sharing faith-insights, praying informally, or experiencing the graces of Scripture together.

Increasingly today we see the proliferation of such groups. The number of charismatics continues to multiply. Marriage Encounter has accomplished much in breaking down walls that prevent communication. Together with the Cursillo movement it has brought a deeper insight into the meaning of the Scriptures for the problems and challenges of daily life. Bible study groups and shared prayer circles are a source of insights no one participant could arrive at alone.

Some who read these lines will have long since found the value of these communal endeavors. Others may regard them with suspicion. But one thing is certain. When people are willing to share their burdens with each other in mutual trust, and in spontaneous prayer to support each other, they are often surprised to find a new purpose and direction in their lives.

To participate in these new movements is not binding on anyone. Nor are they suited to persons with emotional or psychological problems. But if you are reasonably calm and content with life, these new modes of prayer and community offer a genuine means of spiritual growth.

BRINGING OUT YOUR BEST

Why do you need spiritual direction?

To keep you alert to the fact that your Christian vocation implies living not only for yourself but for others.

But this requires a spirit of discernment as to when and how to use the opportunities for service that life presents.

There is a time to correct and a time to heal;
a time to build and a time to stand fast;
a time to speak and a time to be silent.

Authentic spiritual direction will clear your vision for the making of right choices. It will help you understand better your own weaknesses and strengths, and thus enable you to help others as they, in their own way, reach out for a deeper understanding and love of Christ.

Spiritual direction is an important tool for a spirituality suited to today.

The Grace to Heal

Instead, associate with a religious man,
  who you are sure keeps the commandments;
Who is like-minded with yourself
  and will feel for you if you fall. . . .

When a man is wise to his people's
    advantage,
  the fruits of his knowledge are en-
    during. . . .

One wise for himself has full enjoyment,
  and all who see him praise him. . . .

My son, when you are ill, delay not,
  but pray to God, who will heal you:
Flee wickedness; let your hands be just,
  cleanse your heart of every sin. . . .

Then give the doctor his place
  lest he leave; for you need him too.
There are times that give him an advantage,
  and he too beseeches God
That his diagnosis may be correct
  and his treatment bring about a cure.

Sirach 37:12, 22, 24; 38:9-10, 12-14

CHAPTER 7

Spiritual Astronauts

One final characteristic of a spirituality suited to today merits attention. Perhaps, when all is said and done, it is the most important of all.

Let me present it in the form of a riddle.

What essential ingredient of life is highly contagious and spreads like oil on water?

Some further clues: You cannot transfer it by selling it or buying it. It cannot be bought at any price. Everybody needs it as a means of survival itself.

Wise people never hoard it. Wicked people try to kill it. You do not have to be rich to have it, and some rich people do not possess it. When everything else in life fails, it can still be there, if you want it.

The answer, of course, is hope, which may in a special way be called the Easter gift of Christ. In this post-Camelot world, there is a special need for a spirituality that is infused and invigorated by the beliefs that life is worth living and that the world can be made a better place in which to live, if enough of us make use of our God-given opportunities.

The astronauts who explored outer space and landed on the moon had to be men of hope; otherwise they would never have taken the risk of their perilous journeys. When the rockets that carried them rose from their launching pads they had to overcome the tremendous drag of gravity; the first few feet of flight needed the greatest output of power.

It requires spiritual astronauts today — well acquainted with the hazards of the mission but fortified by confidence and a strong desire to succeed — to overcome the drag of pessimism and cynicism that seek to hold them down as they try to lift themselves up and point their flight toward the distant star.

TWO VIEWS OF LIFE

Question: What's the difference between a theologian and a scientist?

Answer: The theologian is an optimist. The scientist is a pessimist.

This, of course, is a gross oversimplification. Without looking too far, we can find cheerful scientists and gloomy theologians. Nevertheless, the answer contains a good-sized nugget of truth.

A few years ago two important meetings, quite diverse in character, took place, one in Europe, the other in the United States. There was a convocation of theologians in Brussels, Belgium, and it received a good deal of attention in the press. They were discussing new trends and new directions in their chosen field.

Not long afterward the annual convention of the Association for the Advancement of Science was held in New York, with well-known scientists presenting learned papers on a variety of topics.

A university professor who attended both of these meetings commented afterward that there was a striking difference in the spirit of the participants.

Hope for the future lived and breathed in the lectures and discussions of the theologians.

For the scientists, the future was bleak, with very little to relieve the gloom of impending disaster.

DISASTER COURSE

If we do not accept the supernatural dimension in the human condition, then indeed it is not difficult to find reasons for gloom and dismay at our present world situation.

For 40 years, continuously, somewhere in the world a war has been in progress. And there seems to be an undeclared war in our city streets, where criminals on the prowl make it unsafe to walk about at night. Shoplifting has become epidemic, and no one really knows how to deal with it, or with the hard-drug users who resort to theft and mugging to support their habit.

Well-known celebrities openly set aside in their sex lives the moral standards held sacred for generations, and blithely advertise their conduct on the TV talk shows.

These are matters of group or individual morality, and they raise the question: Is the fabric of society itself being corroded?

When we look at the way we have treated our planet home no wonder the future seems grim. We have two alternatives, scientists say, and both of them are forbidding. We can continue to waste and destroy our natural resources, pollute the water and atmosphere beyond redemption, and overpopulate beyond the ability of the earth to sustain life.

Or, with the awesome nuclear bombs now available, we can witness a spectacular ending of the human drama, and be part of the action ourselves, when some madman in a position of power pulls the switch that sets off a series of multimegaton explosions, thereby releasing a storm of deadly radioactivity on all living things.

As the grim joke, said to be circulating in Czechoslovakia, expresses it:

"What should you do if an atomic bomb explodes over the city?"

"Don't panic. Simply wrap yourself in a winding sheet and crawl to the nearest cemetery."

HARD CHOICES

No wonder that against this background the scientist asks the theologian: "What is there to be cheerful about?"

Part of the answer lies in the fact that a theologian, by definition, starts out with some basic premises that a sizable number of scientists exclude from their thinking.

Man, created by an all-wise Creator, has it within himself to save himself. God does not provide a blueprint on how atomic power is to be used, just as he did not directly reveal its existence in the first place. Along with the gifts of intelligence and free will there is the corresponding responsibility of careful study, of wise discernment as to the use of newly discovered sources of power, of responsible stewardship of the secrets that the earth is constantly opening up to human ingenuity.

God does not intervene in the choices that we make, but he does provide wisdom and courage for those who have to make these choices, if they humbly ask for these gifts in the spirit of King Solomon 3,000 years ago:

"Give me, therefore, wisdom and knowledge to lead this people, for otherwise who could rule this great people of yours?" (2 Chronicles 1:10)

The late President Kennedy was surely thinking of the prophets of gloom and doom among us when, in a famous speech at American University in 1963, he said:

"Too many of us think peace is impossible. Too many think it is unreal. This is a dangerous, defeatist belief. It leads to the conclusion that war is inevitable, that mankind is doomed, that we are gripped by forces we cannot control. We need not accept that view."

The theologian does not accept it, and in this sense he is an optimist.

Peter Farb, in his intriguing book *Man's Rise to Civilization,* writes about the Natchez Indians, a tribe which died out about the year 1700. They were sun worshipers, and their chief had the title "Brother of the Sun." According to a contemporary account:

"Every morning the great chief honors by his presence the rising of his older brother, and salutes him with many howlings as soon as he appears above the horizon. Afterward, raising his hands above his head, and turning from east to west, he shows him the direction he must take on his course."

For the pessimist, we are as foolish as the Natchez Indians if we think we can do anything about the inevitable disaster, now that scientists have put at our disposal powers of destruction beyond imagination.

But the optimist, even while smiling at the naïveté of the Indians, does not use the word inevitable in considering human potential. He is confident that even the power of the sun can be controlled and harnessed and that humanity is capable of unexpected and surprising nobility.

The theologian is an optimist for another reason. He believes in a God of the living and of the dead, who has imparted to his human creatures, in a mysterious way, the gift of immortality.

For those who do not believe this, the threatened last great atomic blast, destroying all life, must necessarily be equated with pointless darkness and annihilation. For one who believes in survival after death, there is indeed the duty of preserving life, for that is the stewardship that the Creator has entrusted to us. But if by accident or the perverted action of some madman, a vast atomic blast should devastate the world or part of it, beyond such an event, on the word of Christ, lies a new chapter in human existence, one which opens up to immeasurable prospects of joy and further growth.

CHRIST IS RISEN

Gloom and discouragement lay upon the disciples of Christ like a heavy fog after his crucifixion.

Peter, after promising he would lay down his life for Christ, ends up by swearing that he had never known him. Judas had betrayed him and was lost. The other apostles, except for John, had scattered when the soldiers came to take Christ, hiding themselves in fear and trembling.

They had expected the Messiah to throw off his humble ways and at the last moment summon an army to conquer the Roman intruders. And now disaster had struck. Their leader was humiliated and crucified.

"On the evening of that first day of the week, even though the disciples had locked the doors of the place where they were for fear of the Jews, Jesus came and stood before them. 'Peace be with you,' he said. When he had said this, he showed them his hands and his side. At the sight of the Lord the disciples rejoiced. 'Peace be with you,' he said again.

"'As the Father has sent me, so I send you'" (John 20:19-21).

The disciples were filled with joy because once more they had hope. And in the hope that was born that day they confidently went out to win the world for Christ.

There is a saying: Keep your fear to yourself; share your courage with others. This is not the time for a fainthearted and apologetic spirituality. It is not the time to be on the defensive about what we believe. The trumpet call is what the world needs, not a timid murmur of apology.

We must sound out with the vigor of a trumpet call that the great ultimate realities of the faith remain unchanged; they are not affected by the changes in discipline and practice which have come about in this time of renewal.

What are these great central realities?

God does exist. He does love each one of us with an infinite love, and asks us to love one another in his name. He sent his divine Son to redeem us by his Death and Resurrection, and he founded the Church to speak in his name to his followers. He has vested every human person with the responsibility for his or her eternal destiny, and he promises happiness in a life to come to his faithful followers.

HOPE FOR THE FUTURE

Utopia is defined as any condition, place, or situation of social or political perfection. Utopian as an adjective means "excellent or ideal, but existing only in visionary or impractical thought or theory."

The word was invented by St. Thomas More, and it was used as the title of a book that he wrote in the year 1516 about an imaginary island that was described as the seat of perfection in moral, social, and political life.

It would indeed be utopian to suppose that, in the frailty of the human condition, the establishment of perfect peace and harmony is possible. That is reserved for another time and place. The human condition remains pretty much compounded of the elements that it has always possessed: a little unselfishness joined to a great deal of self-serving; pettiness and meanness of spirit, but an occasional outbreak of nobility that sends our spirit soaring.

But it is this last "X-factor" that keeps the ideal alive. The remarkable thing about hope is that it cannot really be killed, unless we personally become its executioner. People have witnessed the loss of their homes, their cities, even their loved ones in earthquakes, floods, and tornadoes, but when we see them being interviewed, standing in the ruins of their homes, it is clear that, even in their state of emotional shock, hope for the future has not been destroyed. They are ready to pick up the pieces and start over.

And this kind of hope is not just wishful thinking. People do start over after catastrophe, and they do succeed. And we surely must have that same determined hope in our spirituality today.

GROWTH IN THE SPIRIT

Several years ago an interviewer asked Cardinal Suenens, internationally known for his positive and progressive spirit, this question:

"Why are you a man of hope, even in these days?"

The prelate replied: "I am hopeful because I believe that the Holy Spirit is still the creating Spirit, and that he will give us every morning fresh freedom, joy and a new provision of hope, if we open our soul to him.

"The story of the Church is a long story, filled with the wonders of the Holy Spirit: We must remember the saints and prophets bringing, in hopeless times, a gulf stream of graces and new light to continue on the road. I believe in the surprises of the Holy Spirit. The Council was such a surprise, and Pope John was another. They took us aback. Why should we think that

God's imagination and love might be exhausted?"

To which we might add: They will not and cannot be exhausted as long as God can find those who are willing to put their talents and abilities into partnership with him. As the sign on my friend's desk put it: Lord, no problem will come up today that you and I cannot solve together.

There are such wonderful potentialities in all of us. God gives us enough graces and abilities to use for many lifetimes.

Circumstances outside ourselves can without doubt influence our lives, but essentially we are molded and shaped from within. No outward circumstance, no matter how unfortunate, can really prevent our growth toward maturity, our progress toward a greater love of God. In fact, they are among the surprises of the Spirit that can make us grow, but only if we are open to those surprises and accept them gratefully.

EASTER PEOPLE

If you have good health, good fortune, and a warm love of family around you, be glad and be grateful, and see in this a foreshadowing of the joy and peace that God has in store for those who love him.

But you do not have a guarantee of such good fortune. It may be that the world has suddenly shown you its ugly side. You have to bear the cross of illness, loneliness, misunderstanding, or financial worry. In your quiet moments of prayer, try to see yourself as one of the fortunates on this earth, called to share in the trials and sufferings of Jesus in St. Paul's daring phrase: ". . . fill up what is lacking in the sufferings of Christ" (Colossians 1:24). You cannot escape the reality of your suffering, but buoyed up by hope you can adjust accordingly and leave no entrance into your heart to discouragement or despair. Indeed, your present problem may well be a non-problem by next year. Or you may find a new window in your soul to admit the sunlight and experience an altogether new kind of joy.

"It will go well with those servants whom the master finds wide-awake on his return. I tell you, he will put on an apron, seat them at table, and proceed to wait on them" (Luke 12:37).

Doesn't that homely and comfortable picture drawn by Christ give you all the grounds you need for hope in your lives? Whatever your present distress, Christ will make it up to you in the end. You have his word.

That is why I end as I began: "You must have hope, you must be an optimist, if your spirituality today is to be genuine and effective."

You can help to change the world and, in the process of doing so, find that something that is really more important has come to pass: You have changed yourself; you have become more mature and open and generous in your relationship with God and with your fellow human beings.

In his Gospel account of Jesus' farewell address to his apostles, St. John has Christ continually returning to one point: "This is my commandment: love one another as I have loved you" (John 15:12). In this you, also, will discover the true Christian life, the fulfillment of all your hopes, a new world of light and peace.

All Things New

"Then I saw new heavens and a new earth.
The former heavens and
   the former earth had passed away,
and the sea was no longer.
I also saw a new Jerusalem, the holy city,
coming down out of heaven from God,
beautiful as a bride prepared
   to meet her husband.
I heard a loud voice from the throne cry out:
'This is God's dwelling among men.
He shall dwell with them
and they shall be his people
and he shall be their God who is
   always with them.
He shall wipe every tear from their eyes,
and there shall be no more death or mourning,
crying out or pain,
for the former world has passed away!'
The One who sat on the throne said to me,
'See, I make all things new! . . .' "

Revelation 21:1-5

Epilogue

"I will give you a new heart and place a new spirit within you, taking from your bodies your stony hearts and giving you natural hearts" (Ezekiel 36:26).

These are the words of the Lord transmitted through Ezekiel the prophet, writing 600 years before Christ. They were addressed to the Jewish exiles in Babylon, driven there by Nebuchadnezzar's army after the crushing defeat of Israel.

It was the prophet's task to keep alive the hope of his discouraged and dejected people. For him, these exiles were the hope of Israel's restoration. Purified and cleansed of their stubborn pride by their sufferings in captivity, they would one day return to their homeland and once more worship the Lord in his temple on Mount Zion.

In Chapter 37 of Ezekiel occurs the celebrated vision of the dry bones covering the ground in a vast plain, where a great battle had taken place; victors and losers were now indistinguishable among the fallen.

"He asked me: Son of man, can these bones come to life? 'Lord God,' I answered, 'you alone know that.'

"I will put my spirit in you that you may live, and I will settle you upon your land; thus you shall know that I am the Lord. I have promised, and I will do it, says the Lord" (Ezekiel 37:3, 14).

HEART AT THE CENTER

The burden of this book has been that the Lord is putting new life into dry bones once more, in our day; and our growth in spirituality depends on how open we are to receive that life-giving word, making it effective for all those whose lives we are destined to influence in some way.

What kind of a person will you be if you respond to the life-giving impulse of the Spirit?

You will be a person who heals, who builds bridges, who makes peace, who speaks often to God in his secret room.

You will be a person with heart.

"You've got to have heart" is the refrain of a once-popular song, witnessing to the need for energy, enthusiasm, a never-say-die spirit. People who lack heart are quickly defeated and cowed in the battles and the storms of life.

It is significant that although physiologically we know very well it is the brain and not the heart that is the center of thought, emotion, and feeling, nevertheless, symbolically, the heart remains in staunch possession of our minds as the symbol of love.

We still find scratched on walls and carved on trees two hearts with an arrow through them. "He surely puts his heart in his work" is a common expression of praise. And if we want to extend sympathy to someone who has suffered a great loss through death, we say: "I want to express my heartfelt sorrow."

The process by which we make decisions depends and should depend (primarily at least) on the head, but neither can one discount the strong influence of the heart. When Cardinal John Henry Newman had convinced himself intellectually that he should enter the Catholic Church, he still delayed his conversion for several years. When a friend asked him one day the reason for the delay his response was: "The heart has reasons of which the head knows nothing."

Newman was surely a precursor of the spirit that moves among us today. On his gravestone he wanted these words inscribed:

"Heart speaks to heart."

REAL PRESENCE

To be a bridgebuilder, healer, a peacemaker, a strong support of our neighbors, we must be present to them with our heart, not merely intellectually and not merely on the physical plane.

To understand the problems of people in an intellectual way does not mean that we are able to reach out to them with the love that they need. That is something the heart must give.

And we can be physically present to people without even adverting to their uniqueness as individuals. Even a corpse can be physically present in a room in this sense.

Or we can be present to each other like unrelated islands. Strangers waiting nervously in a dentist's office are present to each other in this way. They are conscious of the fact that other people are in the room, but each is a self-contained island of personal concern, intent on his or her particular dental problem.

There is a presence which shares a kind of surface enthusiasm. Such can be seen at a football or baseball game, where we are present to each other, but only in common attention to the game in progress, without any interest in our neighbors beyond that.

Then there is the presence of personal interest and concern, giving entire attention even in a short encounter. To act in this way is to affirm the worth of our neighbor. There is no greater gift that we have to offer to anyone than to affirm that person's worth, possessing, as each one does, a uniqueness that is a special gift from God. And conversely, there is no greater sin than not to affirm a person's worth, for this is to blind ourselves to the immediate presence of Christ, who said: "I assure you, as often as you did it for one of my least brothers, you did it for me" (Matthew 25:40). Whether in a planned or casual encounter, it is Christ who stands before us.

WORKING WITH GOD

"I've given up on the institutional church."

Not a few people seem to be saying that in their actions, if not in their words.

Religion has been around a long time, they argue, and look at the state of the world. The followers of Christ don't seem to have accomplished very much in the way of bringing about the reign of peace and justice.

G. K. Chesterton was a British convert who became a vigorous apologist for the faith. He died almost 50 years ago, and his books are somewhat neglected now. But one paradox of his is still widely quoted and deserves to be:

"Christianity hasn't failed; the problem is that it has not yet been seriously tried."

Perhaps we need a new patron saint to prompt us in this area. As a likely candidate, I suggest Lydia. In her house, the Eucharist was shared for the first time (possibly) on European soil; at least, it is the first such European gathering recorded in the Scriptures. And Lydia is the one who made it happen.

Paul, on his first missionary journey, had confined himself to the territory of Asia Minor, now the nation of Turkey. But on his second journey he found himself one day in Troas, or Troy, the ancient city of Homer's *Iliad,* near the western coast of Asia Minor.

There a man appeared to him in his sleep, dressed in the distinctive style of the Macedonians who lived in what is now Greece. He said to Paul: "Come over to Macedonia and help us" (Acts 16:9).

Whether it was a genuine vision or a dream, Paul needed no further sign. He boarded ship and sailed across the Aegean Sea to Greece, where he decided to make his first missionary stop at the city of Philippi.

Then, in just a few lines, the historic meeting with Lydia is described. St. Luke, author of the Acts, is writing as an eyewitness:

"Once, on the sabbath, we went outside the city gate to the bank of the river, where we thought there would be a place of prayer. We sat down and spoke to the women who were gathered there. One who listened was a woman named Lydia, a dealer in purple goods from the town of Thyatira. She already reverenced God, and the Lord opened her heart to accept what Paul was saying. After she and her household had been baptized, she extended us an invitation: 'If you are convinced that I believe in the Lord, come and stay at my house.' She managed to prevail on us'' (Acts 16:13-15).

Who was this Lydia?

A dye maker, as the Jerusalem Bible expresses it. Apparently, her husband, if she had been married, was dead. But it seems that she had prospered in her business of producing the rich purple dye, made from mollusks gathered on the shore of the Aegean Sea and much favored by the fashionable world. She had a large home and servants and friends who admired her.

But something was missing in her life, and she prayed to a God she scarcely knew. Her heart was open to receive the saving Word and the light of God's truth.

When the Word and the light came to her through Paul, she joyfully and gratefully accepted it. In a true sense, she was a pioneer and a bridgebuilder for all of us in the Western World.

Lydia and the Christians of Philippi became very dear to the heart of Paul. From Rome he addressed them tenderly:

"You whom I so love and long for, you who are my joy and my crown" (Philippians 4:1).

UNFULFILLED POTENTIAL

Paul and Lydia can encourage us to joyful faith and optimistic trust in Christ. And they have their modern counterpart in that prince of optimists, Pope John. There is a saying ascribed to him that puts in capsule form the message of this book:

"Consult not your fears, but your hopes and your dreams.

"Think not about your frustrations, but about your unfulfilled potential.

"Concern yourself not with what you tried and failed in, but with what it is still possible for you to do."

Frank Sheed, writer and publisher to whom the Church owes a great debt for his own eloquent optimism about the value and validity of the Christian message, related in one of his syndicated columns a story they tell in Ireland.

A holy man of God met our Lady with her Child in a solitary glen in the wild country south of Dublin.

And the Blessed Mother, showing herself Irish, at least by adoption, greeted him with these lilting phrases:

"I am the Mother of God and this is himself, and he is the Boy you will all be wanting at the last."

Continuing the Irish lilt:

May you recognize your need for Christ first, last, and always; and may the light shine out of the two eyes of you, like a candle set in two windows of the house, bidding the wanderer to come in out of the storm.

For there is indeed a storm, and there are indeed wanderers, looking for a secure home and a place where the loneliness in their lives can be healed by love. And you and I and all of us have the power to reflect for them the love of Christ.

And this is the love that all of us will be wanting at the last.